The Temporality of Festivals

CHRONOI
Zeit, Zeitempfinden, Zeitordnungen
Time, Time Awareness, Time Management

—

Edited by

Eva Cancik-Kirschbaum, Christoph Markschies and Hermann Parzinger

on behalf of Einstein Center Chronoi

Volume 10

The Temporality of Festivals

Approaches to Festive Time in Ancient Babylon, Greece, Rome, and Medieval China

Edited by
Anke Walter

DE GRUYTER

ISBN 978-3-11-136486-5
e-ISBN (PDF) 978-3-11-136687-6
e-ISBN (EPUB) 978-3-11-136770-5
ISSN 2701-1453
DOI https://doi.org/10.1515/9783111366876

This work is licensed under the Creative Commons Attribution-NonCommercial-NoDerivatives 4.0 International License. For details go to https://creativecommons.org/licenses/by-nc-nd/4.0/. Creative Commons license terms for re-use do not apply to any content (such as graphs, figures, photos, excerpts, etc.) that is not part of the Open Access publication. These may require obtaining further permission from the rights holder. The obligation to research and clear permission lies solely with the party re-using the material.

Library of Congress Control Number: 2023952466

Bibliographic information published by the Deutsche Nationalbibliothek
The Deutsche Nationalbibliothek lists this publication in the Deutsche Nationalbibliografie; detailed bibliographic data are available on the Internet at http://dnb.dnb.de.

© 2024 with the author(s), editing © 2024 Anke Walter published by Walter de Gruyter GmbH, Berlin/Boston. The book is published open access at www.degruyter.com.

Printing and binding: CPI books GmbH, Leck

www.degruyter.com

Table of Contents

Anke Walter
Introduction —— 1

John Steele
Astronomical, Sequential, and Festive Time in the Late Babylonian New Year Festival —— 11

Glenn W. Most
"The Tragic Day" —— 27

Anke Walter
Festive Time in the Poetry of Horace —— 39

Alain Arrault
Recovering Memory by Cumulating Calendars: Festivities at Dunhuang in Medieval China (9th–10th Centuries) —— 59

Index —— 93

Anke Walter
Introduction

How can time become festive? How do festivals, in the constant stream of time, manage to make time "special", to mark out a certain day or days, to distinguish them from "normal", everyday time, and to fill them with meaning – a meaning that can encompass the past, the present, and the future? And how can we reconstruct what festive time looked like in the past and what people thought about it? While a lot of research has been done on festivals from the point of view of several scholarly disciplines,[1] the specific temporality of festivals has not yet attracted sufficient attention. In this small volume, scholars from different fields will provide answers to the questions raised above, with particular focus on whether and how we can recover a sense of the temporality of festivals of the past, through calendars and other sources, but also through literature, with its own complex constructions of time. As we shall see, cultures as diverse as ancient Babylon, Greece and Rome, and medieval China all share a sense of calendrically recurring festive time as something special that needs to be carefully mapped out and preserved, often with great sophistication, and that gives us precious insights into the broader religious, political, and social dimensions of time in the cultures of the past.

Among the many angles that have been taken in the scholarship on festive days, an approach that foregrounds the distinction between "the everyday" and "the festive" ("Alltag" and "Fest") is particularly helpful for our purposes.[2] An important qualification needs to be made at this point: the focus of this volume are the – mostly religious – festivals that have a firm place in the calendar and that keep returning at regular intervals, usually every year.[3] This means that private

---

[1] An overview of the different approaches that have been taken can be found in the collected volumes edited by Bianco and Del Ninno (1981); Schultz (1988); Haug and Warning (1989); Maurer (2004a).
[2] See already Durkheim (1912) for the distinction between religious and profane time; Pieper (1963a, esp. 5–13); Martin (1973, esp. 36–41); Marquard (1988, esp. 414–415); Assmann (1989a, esp. 243); Maurer (2004c, 23–26); see also, from a slightly different perspective, Ratschow (1991, 239–240) on the interplay between festivals and the passage of time.
[3] Cf. the distinction between "Fest" and "Feier" introduced by Bollnow (1955): a 'Fest' is a recurrent, natural phenomenon, which is usually a joyful occasion. A 'Feier' is held at irregular intervals, it is historical rather than natural, and establishes historical meaning. It is generally solemn in character. On this distinction, see also Gebhardt (1987); Martin (1973, 74–76); Deile (2004, 13–17); Maurer (2004c, 32); Homann (2004, esp. 108–110). Cf. however Maurer's criticism of this distinction as not sufficiently strict in reality and grounded in linguistic practice: Maurer (2004c, 37); Pieper (1963a, 52).

Open Access. © 2024 the author(s), published by De Gruyter. This work is licensed under the Creative Commons Attribution-NonCommercial-NoDerivatives 4.0 International License.
https://doi.org/10.1515/9783111366876-001

or public celebrations, such as baptisms, weddings, or triumphs will not be part of the discussion. What interests us here is the festive time that is mandated by the calendar: the festive days that recur regularly, turning everyday time into festive time again and again, not because something special has just happened – such as a military victory to be celebrated with a triumph – but because the time for a certain festival that was instituted in the past has come round again. The most fundamental tool for determining these are different kinds of calendars as well as astronomical calculations, which announce the coming of a specific festival, such as the new year festival that is discussed by both John Steele for ancient Babylon and Alain Arrault for medieval China in this volume.

Most of the festivals studied here are primarily religious in nature, but they can have a political dimension as well. The question of who declares a day to be a festival, who has an interest in upholding certain festive traditions, and how much time is accorded to certain kinds of festive activities can be intimately connected with questions of power and authority, both religious and political.[4] The Babylonian new year festival examined by John Steele is a very good example of the way both spheres are connected, and of the role astronomical calculations play for both – to the point where the language used for astronomical accounts begins to coincide with the language of "short-time" ritual prescriptions, in an intriguing "astralization" of ritual. Classical Athens too and the way the tragic competitions (*agones*) are embedded in the religious and political life of the city (*polis*), discussed by Glenn Most in this volume, makes this multidimensional meaning of festive time very clear. Similarly, the Roman poet Horace is acutely aware of both the distinction and the interplay of festive time as experienced in the private realm and the temporality of official, public celebration, and integrates the tension between them into his corpus of odes. At the same time, as Alain Arrault shows in his contribution, festivity can also be a means of transgressing the boundaries between different social classes, ethnicities, and religious groups: in medieval Dunhuang, at least, festivals were by no means restricted to individual groups, but we need to cumulate different festive calendars to gain a sense of what festive time really looked like for the members of a community, as well as when and how often it came about.

While calendars seem to offer neat demarcations of festive time – from the beginning of a day with midnight, sunrise, or sunset, to the end of that day or a couple of days – festive time is actually a bit harder to define. It tends to spill

---

[4] For the political side of festivals, which represent and enact existing power relationships, fixing a certain interpretation of the past and a resulting agenda for the future (cf. e.g. national festivals), see especially Maurer (2004c, 48–51) with p. 51 n. 78 for further literature on festivals in the former GDR and under the NS regime; see also Pieper (1963a, 20–25) for the French Revolution.

over, as it were, into the time of everyday life: especially for elaborate festivities, preparations often need to start early on, as decorations need to be produced, music and dances need to be rehearsed, food needs to be prepared. They allow the participants to anticipate the festive time, and they might become little festivals or events in themselves. Similarly, there is usually no strict end to festive time: there might still be leftover festive food for a couple of days, festive tunes might still be in our ear, decorations need to be taken down and clothing washed and carefully stored, in anticipation of the next iteration of the festivities. Little islands of festive time, then, tend to dot everyday life too, both before and after the festivities themselves.

Not only the external or internal markers of festive time distinguish the temporality of festivals from the temporality of everyday life, but also what is contained in this festive time frame – what fills festive time. The characteristic temporality of festivals has been studied by Hans-Georg Gadamer, in his philosophical exploration of art and the proper time ("Eigenzeit") of artworks.[5] For him, festivals are characterized by the community of those gathered, with a shared intention and focus. Both festive speech and silence are features of festivals, which, in their recurrence, have their own time ("Eigenzeit"): a festival is not empty time that people themselves have to fill, but when a festival arrives and time becomes festive, the festival "fills time", just as it arrests time and makes it linger. Time is no longer subject to our planning and disposition ("Das scheint mir nun auch für das Fest charakteristisch, dass es durch seine eigene Festlichkeit Zeit vorgibt und damit Zeit anhält und zum Verweilen bringt – das ist das Feiern. Der berechnende, disponierende Charakter, in dem man sonst über seine Zeit verfügt, wird im Feiern sozusagen zum Stillstand gebracht.") – much as the artwork, which has its own temporal structure, which it imposes upon those who engage with it.[6]

This creates an intriguing simultaneity of two layers of time. On the one hand, even during a festival, life is still regulated by the same kind of clock as always and still measured in minutes and hours. Our bodies are still subject to the rhythm of their normal physiological processes (although festivals might substantially interfere with our regular routines of eating and being hungry, of sleeping and being awake). And yet, time might still be perceived differently during a festival: as passing very quickly, because of the excitement of the festivities and the distractions they offer – especially if a festival is connected with agonistic games with their own excitement and agonistic sense of time – or very slowly, for instance when

---

5 Gadamer (²2020).
6 Gadamer (²2020, 64–69), quote from p. 69.

an unusual sense of peace and quiet sets in, one that might even make one think that the passage of time has been halted, at least for a little while.

The question of festive time perception is connected with the fact that the time of the festival might be filled with unusual activities: rituals that are performed only, say, once a year,[7] the preparation and serving of special food, the getting-together of groups of people who might not normally interact in person in everyday life. This festive interruption of the regular rhythms of time, however, need not always be seen in a positive light. Galen, for instance, from a medical point of view, rejects such irregular, man-made interventions in the natural passage of time, due to human convention or religious observation, as having a potentially disruptive effect on human behaviour and the regular routines that are conducive to good health.[8]

In spiritual terms, however, the special function of festive time has been discussed from a number of angles. Most importantly, different thoughts and conversations often fill festive time. Gerhard Martin, for instance, argues that "festive time", as opposed to "working time" ("Festzeit" vs. "Arbeitszeit") broadens the consciousness and the mind ("Bewusstseinserweiterung"), which leads to an enhanced experience of life in every respect.[9] Harvey Cox goes in a similar direction, singling out three main characteristics of festivities: conscious excess, celebrative affirmation, and "juxtaposition", most importantly with everyday life. All three dimensions together allow men "to keep alive to time by relating past, present, and future to each other".[10]

The commemorative function of festivals has been well examined by Jan Assmann, who shows that the celebration of festive days has an essential function for

---

[7] For the ritual aspects of festivity from the point of view of cultural anthropology, see Turner (1984); Turner and Turner (1984); Bell (1997, esp. 102–108; 120–128); Droogers (2001). For the connection between festivals, rituals, and games or play, see Martin (1973, 66–74); Maurer (2004c, 38–42).
[8] Singer (2022, 33–34).
[9] Martin (1973, esp. 49–53); see also Kerényi (1952); Leppin (2004, 86–88); Albrecht (2000, 371–376) on how festivals allow us to gain an overview over the world and provide orientation in life, which can then be fully embraced.
[10] Cox (1969, 7–55, quote from p. 23). In theological terms, Leppin (2004, 83–86) emphasizes that festivals remind men of the "non-availability" ("Unverfügbarkeit") of human existence. By contrast, Pieper (1963a); Pieper (1963b); Albrecht (2000, 366–368); Deile (2004, 7) interpret festivals as affirmative of life ("lebensbejahend"), as confirming man's place within the world created by God. – For the connection of festivals with excess, see Freud (1912/13, 425); Küchenhoff (1989, 102); Köpping (1997); Albrecht (2000, 368–370). For carnivalesque festivals and their relationship with social and moral order, see Davis (1975, 97–123); Abrahams and Baumann (1978); Ladurie (1979, esp. 337–359); Bakhtin (1984, esp. 244–277).

what he terms "cultural memory" ("kulturelles Gedächtnis"[11]). Taking his cue from the difference between everyday life and festivals, he argues that everyday life is characterized by the three features of "contingency", "scarcity", and "routine": by accidents and unforeseeable events, as well as a certain arbitrariness and lack of structure; by economic scarcity, which necessitates work, division of labour, and order, but which is also characterized by a lack of meaning; and the automatization, habitualization, and banality of everyday life routines. The festival, by contrast, is not contingent, but "staged" or "enacted" ("inszeniert"), i.e., it is not subject to accident, it is structured and non-arbitrary; it is characterized by abundance rather than scarcity and by the transcendence of the narrow perspective of everyday life and its routines, the thinking in larger, cosmic contexts and the "effervescence" of emotions – all hallmarks of beauty and completeness, which humans need, but which cannot be realized within the constraints of everyday life. The festival, according to Assmann, embodies and enacts the "other time", the time that goes beyond the "now" of everyday life, that establishes a connection with the dead, the cosmos, the foundational past.[12] To the extent that the latter are all objects of "cultural" versus "communicative memory" (which is more closely linked to everyday life), festivals are the most original and the central instantiation of "cultural memory". They allow humans to be "two-dimensional", i.e., to live in two spheres of time at once.[13]

In a very comprehensive way, then, festive time is closely connected with everyday time, beyond the more practical aspects like the preparations for and the aftermath of festivals that also bind the two together. If, as Assmann shows, what happens during a festival informs our thinking and understanding of ourselves as human beings "in time", that will inform our everyday life as well: we might, after a festival, have a stronger sense of perspective and purpose, one that might be refreshed, as it were, in regular intervals whenever it is again time for festivity. Similarly, the regular intervals of festive time allow participants to trace their own lifetime, from childhood over adolescence to old age, as well as the developments of nations or communities, even while the continuity of certain traditions, values, or beliefs is reaffirmed.

Festive time, even that of our present, is a complex phenomenon that has many different facets. How, do we get access to the festive time of the past?

---

11 On which, see e.g. Assmann and Harth (1991); Assmann (1992); Assmann (1999); Assmann (2000).
12 On this aspect, see also Eliade (1965); Eliade (^{2}1969); Albert (1967). Kerényi (1952, esp. 61–66) sees "the essence of festivity' ("das Wesen des Festes") in the fact that it allows humans to partake in the creation of the world.
13 See Assmann (1991); also Assmann (1989b); Maurer (2004b).

Which traces does the recurring, yet ephemeral celebration of festivals leave for later generations? To start with, calendars are a key tool not only for regulating a community"s festive life, but also for transmitting the festive rhythm to future generations. As Alain Arrault shows in this volume, different temporal dimensions come into play here as calendars can prescribe festive time for the future or chronicle it after the event. Yet the calendrical definition of festive time risks being too narrow, and it risks overlooking all those aspects that make the study of the temporality of festivals so complex and rewarding. For in addition to time-measuring devices such as calendars, all different kinds of items that are used only at specific times of the year on festive occasions, such as sacred objects, or special clothes and decorations, but also wine, music, and dance, can help mark time out as festive and make the special character of a designated festive time span felt by those involved. Space has a role to play here as well, as everyday spaces, such as the market place, can be transformed into a festive site, or as special spaces can be used during the time of a festival, or a mixture of both could be the case. Together, all these factors create what is perhaps the most powerful marker of festive time, but what is even more intangible: a festive atmosphere that can take hold of the participants for all or parts of the festivities, that can exist in some years, but not in others, and that need not engulf all participants to the same degree. Festive time, then, is not merely a matter of an entry in the calendar, but it has to be understood as a multi-dimensional phenomenon that encompasses many aspects, material and immaterial, objective and importantly also subjective that, in and by themselves, may have little to do with time itself, including space or certain objects.

As we shall see in this volume, while calendars are often preserved that tell us which festivals were celebrated at what time, some of those other, less tangible aspects of festive time tend not to leave a trace in the historical record – this is certainly the case for the Babylonian festivals discussed by John Steele in this volume, for which all that we have is the astronomical record, and which might not even have been celebrated any longer by the time when these records were produced – records that still, however, provide very intriguing insights into the understanding and structuring of festive time in the past. When turning our attention to Chinese festivals, by contrast, the very calendars, when carefully combined and not merely read in isolation, can furnish very vivid information about the character of a specific festive time and the paraphernalia used to mark it out as something special, such as the gifts, sacrifices, and prizes to be won in festive games, as Alain Arrault shows.

Finally, literature too has a special, and often very close, relationship with festive time and provides a special kind of access to festivities of the past – in a medium that has its own conventions for the construction of (literary) time and its own aspirations to artistic timelessness. The key example of "festive" literature in ancient Greece, discussed by Glenn Most in this volume, are the festivals of the Greater Dionysia in Classical Athens, which provided the occasion for the agonistic performance of tragedies and satyr plays, most famously by playwrights such as Aeschylus, Sophocles, and Euripides. As Glenn Most shows, there is an intriguing and very close connection between the passage of the "tragic day" when the tragedies were performed in a festive context and the sense of temporality – focused on the one decisive "tragic day" – within the plays themselves. Moving on to ancient Rome, we see, in Anke Walter"s paper, that the poetry of Horace provides a lens on yet another facet of festive time, from the point of view of lyric poetry. Horace gives us a glimpse of some of the objects that must have marked out festive time for the Romans, such as wine, altars, and garlands. At the same time, his festive poetry reflects also other, material and immaterial, elements that made time festive as well: the company of guests, the laying aside of one"s daytime cares and troubles, and an enhanced sense of the fleetingness and preciousness of the present moment, which is part of the short and equally fleeting life of man. Like calendars, literature too can give us access to the festive temporality of the past, while adding its own, specific literary sense of time to it: as literary works that might reflect and that are written for a specific moment and a specific audience, but that have their own immortal afterlife as a written artifact in view as well.

Festive time, then, is a complex phenomenon that has many different dimensions, forms and functions. When talking about the temporality of past festivity, as we do in this volume, we need to keep in mind the potential, but also the limitations and the kind of the source material at our disposal – calendars tell a different festive story from literature, and Greek tragedy conveys a different sense of time from Roman lyric poetry. Together, the contributions to this volume aim to show that the temporality of festivals can be a valuable and powerful category when approaching the past of cultures as diverse as those of ancient Babylon, Greece, Rome, and medieval China. Obviously, the study of festive time could still be extended much further, comprising the study of religious and political festivals that are still being celebrated today, of a festive temporality that we can still partake in when the time comes, for instance in the Christian, Jewish, Islamic, or other religions.[14] For now, however, this volume specifically focuses on how to reconstruct and understand festive time in different cultures of the past, in the hope

---

[14] The following are good starting points: Post et al. (2001); Ebner et al. (2004); Tuckett (2009); Bieritz (^{3}2014) for Christian, Müller and Dschulnigg (2002); Galley (2003) for Jewish, Schimmel (2001) for Islamic festivals.

of providing a starting point for further work on festive time across different cultures, religions, and disciplinary boundaries.[15]

References

Abrahams, Roger D., and Richard Baumann. 1978. "Ranges of Festival Behaviour." In: *The Reversible World. Symbolic Inversion in Art and Society*, edited by Barbara A. Babcock, 193–208. Ithaca: Cornell University Press.
Albert, Karl. 1967. "Metaphysik des Festes." *Zeitschrift für Religion und Geistesgeschichte* 19:140–152.
Albrecht, Christian. 2000. "Sinnvergewisserung im Distanzgewinn. Liturgische Erwägungen über das Wesen des evangelischen Gottesdienstes zwischen Feier und Fest." *ZThK* 97:362–384.
Assmann, Aleida. 1989a. "Festen und Fasten. Zur Kulturgeschichte und Krise des bürgerlichen Festes." In *Das Fest*, edited by Walter Haug and Rainer Warning, 227–246. Munich: Fink.
Assmann, Aleida. 1999. *Erinnerungsräume. Formen und Wandlungen des kulturellen Gedächtnisses*. Munich: C. H. Beck.
Assmann, Aleida, and Dietrich Harth, eds. 1991. *Mmemosyne. Formen und Funktionen der kulturellen Erinnerung*. Frankfurt: Fischer.
Assmann, Jan. 1989b. "Der schöne Tag: Sinnlichkeit und Vergänglichkeit im altägyptischen Fest." In *Das Fest*, edited by Walter Haug and Rainer Warning, 3–28. Munich: Fink.
Assmann, Jan. 1991. "Der zweidimensionale Mensch: Das Fest als Medium des kollektiven Gedächtnisses." In *Das Fest und das Heilige. Religiöse Kontrapunkte zur Alltagswelt*, edited by Jan Assmann and Theo Sundermeier, 13–33. Gütersloh: Gütersloher Verlagshaus G. Mohn.
Assmann, Jan. 1992. *Das kulturelle Gedächtnis. Schrift, Erinnerung und politische Identität in frühen Hochkulturen*. Munich: C. H. Beck.
Assmann, Jan. 2000. *Religion und kulturelles Gedächtnis. Zehn Studien*. Munich: C. H. Beck.
Bakhtin, Mikhail M. 1984. *Rabelais and His World*. Bloomington: Indiana University Press.
Bell, Catherine M. 1997. *Ritual. Perspectives and Dimensions*. Oxford: Oxford University Press.
Bianco, Carla, and Maurizio Del Ninno, eds. 1981. *Festa. Antropologia e semiotica. Relazioni presentate al Convegno di studi "forme e pratiche della festa"*. Florence: Nuova Guaraldi.
Bieritz, Karl-Heinz. ⁹2014. *Das Kirchenjahr. Feste, Gedenk- und Feiertage in Geschichte und Gegenwart*. Neu bearbeitet von Christian Albrecht. Munich: C. H. Beck.
Bollnow, Otto Friedrich. 1955. *Neue Geborgenheit. Das Problem einer Überwindung des Existentialismus*. Stuttgart: Kohlhammer.
Cox, Harvey. 1969. *The Feast of Fools. A Theological Essay on Festivity and Fantasy*. Cambridge, MA: Harvard University Press.
Davis, Natalie Zemon. 1975. *Society and Culture in Early Modern France*. Stanford: Stanford University Press.
Deile, Lars. 2004. "Feste – eine Definition." In *Das Fest. Beiträge zu seiner Theorie und Systematik*, edited by Michael Maurer, 1–17. Cologne: Böhlau.

---

[15] I very gratefully acknowledge the support for this project from the Einstein Center Chronoi. I am much obliged to the Center for their generosity and hospitality on several occasions. I also acknowledge my affiliation with Newcastle University and, as Extraordinary Researcher, with North-West University, Potchefstroom.

Droogers, André. 2001. "Feasts: A view from cultural anthropology." In *Christian Feast and Festival. The Dynamics of Western Liturgy and Culture*, edited by Paul Post, Gerard Rouwhorst, Louis van Tongeren, and Anton Scheer, 79–96. Leuven: Peeters.
Durkheim, Émile. 1912. *Les formes élémentaires de la vie religieuse. Le système totémique en Australie*. Paris: Félix Alcan.
Ebner, Martin, Fischer, Irmgard, Frey, Jörg, Fuchs, Ottmar, and Berndt Hamm, eds. 2004. *Das Fest. Jenseits des Alltags*. Neukirchen-Vluyn: Neukirchener Verlag.
Eliade, Mircea. 1965. *Le sacré et le profane*. Paris: Gallimard.
Eliade, Mircea. ²1969. *Le mythe de l'éternel retour: archétypes et répétition*. Paris: Gallimard.
Freud, Sigmund. 1912/13. *Totem und Tabu. Einige Übereinstimmungen im Seelenleben der Wilden und der Neurotiker*. Aachen: Hugo Heller & Cie.
Gadamer, Hans-Georg. ²2020. *Die Aktualität des Schönen. Kunst als Spiel, Symbol und Fest*. Stuttgart: Reclam.
Galley, Susanne. 2003. *Das jüdische Jahr. Feste, Gedenk- und Feiertage*. Munich: C. H. Beck.
Gebhardt, Winfried. 1987. *Fest, Feier und Alltag. Über die gesellschaftliche Wirklichkeit des Menschen und ihre Deutung*. Frankfurt: Lang.
Haug, Walter, and Rainer Warning, eds. 1989. *Das Fest*. Munich: Fink.
Homann, Harald. 2004. "Soziologische Ansätze einer Theorie des Festes." In *Das Fest. Beiträge zu seiner Theorie und Systematik*, edited by Michael Maurer, 95–113. Cologne: Böhlau.
Kerényi, Karl. 1952. "Vom Wesen des Festes." In *Die antike Religion. Ein Entwurf von Grundlinien*, edited by Karl Kerényi, 45–70. Düsseldorf: Eugen Diederichs Verlag.
Köpping, Klaus-Peter. 1997. "Fest." In *Vom Menschen. Handbuch Historische Anthropologie*, edited by Christoph Wulf, 1048–1065. Weinheim: Beltz.
Küchenhoff, Joachim. 1989. "Das Fest und die Grenzen des Ichs – Begrenzung und Entgrenzung im "vom Gesetz gebotenen Exzeß"." In *Das Fest*, edited by Walter Haug and Rainer Warning, 99–119. Munich: Fink.
Ladurie, Emmanuel LeRoy. 1979. *Le Carnaval de Romans. De la Chandeleur au mercredi des Cendres 1579-1580*. Paris: Gallimard.
Leppin, Volker. 2004. "Theologische Ansätze einer Theorie des Festes." In *Das Fest. Beiträge zu seiner Theorie und Systematik*, edited by Michael Maurer, 81–93. Cologne: Böhlau.
Marquard, Odo. 1988. "Kleine Philosophie des Festes." In *Das Fest: eine Kulturgeschichte von der Antike bis zur Gegenwart*, edited by Uwe Schultz, 413–420. Munich: Beck.
Martin, Gerhard M. 1973. *Fest und Alltag – Bausteine zu einer Theorie des Festes*. Stuttgart: Kohlhammer.
Maurer, Michael, ed. 2004a. *Das Fest. Beiträge zu seiner Theorie und Systematik*. Cologne: Böhlau.
Maurer, Michael. 2004b. "Feste zwischen Memoria und Exzess. Kulturwissenschaftliche und psychoanalytische Ansätze einer Theorie des Festes." In *Das Fest. Beiträge zu seiner Theorie und Systematik*, edited by Michael Maurer, 115–134. Cologne: Böhlau.
Maurer, Michael. 2004c. "Prolegomena zu einer Theorie des Festes." In *Das Fest. Beiträge zu seiner Theorie und Systematik*, edited by Michael Maurer, 19–54. Cologne: Böhlau.
Müller, Ilse, and Peter Dschulnigg. 2002. *Jüdische und christliche Feste*. Würzburg: Echter.
Pieper, Josef. 1963a. *Über das Phänomen des Festes*. Köln: VS Verlag für Sozialwissenschaften.
Pieper, Josef. 1963b. *Zustimmung zur Welt. Eine Theorie des Festes*. Munich: Kösel.
Post, Paul, Rouwhorst, Gerard, van Tongeren, Louis, and Anton Scheer. 2001. *Christian Feast and Festival. The Dynamics of Western Liturgy and Culture*. Leuven: Peeters.

Ratschow, Carl Heinz. 1991. "Die Feste. Inbegriff sittlicher Gestalt." In *Das Fest und das Heilige. Religiöse Kontrapunkte zur Alltagswelt*, edited by Jan Assmann and Theo Sundermeier, 234–246. Gütersloh: Gütersloher Verlagshaus G. Mohn.

Schimmel, Annemarie. 2001. *Das islamische Jahr. Zeiten und Feste*. Munich: C. H. Beck.

Schultz, Uwe, ed. 1988. *Das Fest: eine Kulturgeschichte von der Antike bis zur Gegenwart*. Munich: C. H. Beck.

Singer, Peter. 2022. *Time for the Ancients. Measurement, Theory, Experience*. Berlin: De Gruyter.

Tuckett, Christopher, ed. 2009. *Feasts and Festivals*. Leuven: Peeters.

Turner, Victor W., ed. 1984. *Celebration. Studies in Festivity and Ritual*. Washington, DC: Smithsonian Institute Press.

Turner, Victor W., and Edith L. B. Turner. 1984. "Religious Celebrations." In *Celebration. Studies in Festivity and Ritual*, edited by Victor W. Turner, 201–219. Washington, DC: Smithsonian Institute Press.

John Steele
Astronomical, Sequential, and Festive Time in the Late Babylonian New Year Festival

Time interacts with festivals and rituals in a variety of ways.[1] Two of the most common are in the scheduling of the festival, both at the level of specifying the day or days on which it will occur by means of a calendar of cultic activities and the timing of the individual rituals and other activities at specific moments within those days, and the ways in which time is experienced by the festival's participants, who, depending upon their various roles as active participants or as audience to the festival, may experience the flow of time differently. Time, of course, is also related to astronomy: the cycles of the moon and sun define the calendar and short time measurements and indications often incorporate astronomical knowledge.

The aim of this study is to explore the roles of various different kinds of time within one particular festival: the Late Babylonian new year festival.[2] This festival represents the final stage of a long tradition of festivals marking the beginning of the new year in Babylonia and Assyria (see Fig. 1 for the geography of the region). This tradition can be traced back to at least the third millennium BCE, probably earlier. Broadly speaking, the Babylonian festival celebrated the beginning of the new year, which is connected to the re-establishment of cosmic order, and the symbolic renewal of the bond between the king, the gods, and the country.[3] In most periods, the festival lasted for around a dozen days, beginning on the first day of Nisannu, the first month of the year. Over the course of the festival, the statues of the major gods would travel to the Esagila temple in Babylon from their shrines in Borsippa and other cities, the king would be sent to the *akītu* house outside of the city walls where he would be ritually cleansed, the creation epic *Enūma Eliš*

---

[1] For the purposes of this study, I use the term "festival" to refer to an organized social activity comprising a series of rituals, at least some part of which have a public component. In doing so, I draw a distinction between regular ritual practice, which takes place only within the confines of the temple and from which the general population were excluded (and probably largely unaware of when and what was happening), and festivals, which, while still being run and controlled by the temple, were community-wide activities. My use of the term is similar to how it is defined by Bidmead (2002, 12–13), who draws on the definition of a festival by Falassi (1967).
[2] The Late Babylonian period refers roughly to the second half of the first millennium BCE, a period when Babylonia was no longer under native rule, being instead ruled successively by the Persians, the Greeks, and the Parthians.
[3] For detailed studies of the new year festival and its parts, see, for example, Pallis (1926), Pongratz-Leisten (1994), Bidmead (2002), and Debourse (2022).

would be recited, and finally the king would return to the Esagila. A remarkable feature of the festival is the ritual humiliation of the king, whose face is slapped by the high priest and who is required to kneel before the statues of the gods. Whilst some elements of the festival are performed inside of the temple, out of general view, other parts, including the processions of the statues of the gods and of the king to and from the *akītu* house were conducted in the open.[4] Indeed, the procession of the statues of the gods was probably one of the only times during the year when they could be seen by the general populace.

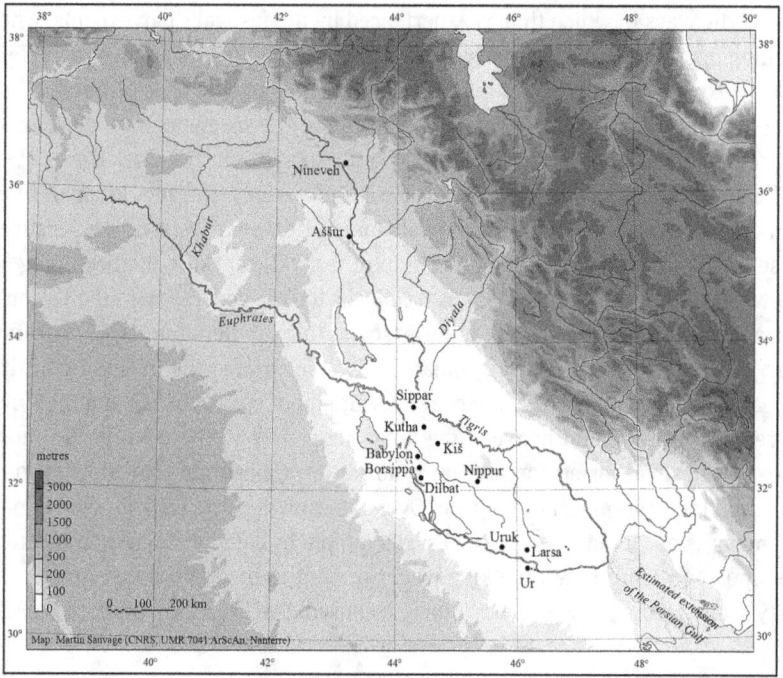

Fig. 1: Map of Babylonia and Assyria during the first millennium BCE. Image credit: Martin Sauvage.

As recently highlighted by Debourse (2022), almost all of the evidence for the new year festival during the Late Babylonian period comes from a series of ritual texts. These texts are scholarly productions, describing the different ritual stages of the

---

[4] At least in earlier periods, the festival was also known as the *akītu* festival in reference to the house in which the king was sequestered. There was also in some times and places a second *akītu* festival at the start of the seventh month, marking the beginning of the second half of the year.

festival and the actions to be undertaken by the priests and other participants within each step. Two groups of texts can be distinguished based upon their provenance: seven texts from Babylon and five from Uruk.[5] The contents of these two groups of texts differ considerably. For example, different gods are mentioned in the Babylon and Uruk texts, the cultic topology differs, and some of the Uruk texts refer to a festival in the seventh month of the year rather than the first month. Most importantly for our purposes, the Uruk texts do not include the same density and specificity of references to time as the texts from Babylon. The festival that is described in the texts from Babylon, which will be the focus of this study, is somewhat different to the new year festival as it can be reconstructed in earlier periods. In particular, there is no reference to the *akītu* house in the preserved fragments (Debourse 2022), suggesting that the procession of the king and his sequestering in that house, which is often assumed to be a defining element of the festival itself, had been eliminated in the late period. Debourse (2022) has further emphasized that we have very little contemporary evidence that the festival even took place at all in this late period. If it did, it may only have been irregular, and was almost certainly a much smaller event than in earlier times. These points are worth remembering in what follows: my discussion of the new year festival is really a discussion of the new year festival as presented in a small group of scholarly ritual texts and may bear little resemblance to the festival as it took place in practice, if, indeed, it did take place.

The New Year Festival as Described in Late Babylonian Ritual Texts from Babylon

Seven tablets are known which contain descriptions of parts of the new year festival at Babylon (see Fig. 2). Four of these are large, detailed accounts of one or more days of the festival;[6] the three other tablets contain material relating to particular aspects of the festival.[7] The fragments preserve parts of the descriptions of the second to the fifth days of Nisannu, the first month of the year. Texts concerning the first day, which is presumed to be the beginning of the festival, and the

---

5 For the texts from Babylon, see below. For the texts from Uruk, see Linssen (2004, 184–214).
6 These four tablets are DT 15, DT 114, BM 32485 + DT 109, and MNB 1848. A composite edition and translation of these texts is presented in Linssen (2004, 215–237); editions and translations of the individual tablets are given by Debourse (2022, 94–160).
7 These three tablets are BM 41577, BM 32655, and BM 32374. Editions and translations of these texts are given by Debourse (2022, 160–176).

sixth day onwards have not been identified, although a few references to coming events which are to take place between the sixth and the twelfth day are mentioned in the descriptions of the second to fifth day.[8]

Activities during the second to the fourth days of the new year festival (and probably also on the first day) take place fully within the confines of the Esagila temple. The Esagila was the main temple in Babylon dedicated to Marduk, the patron god of the city of Babylon and hero of the Babylon-centred creation epic *Enūma Eliš*, and therefore the most important temple within the city. For these days the texts centre on the actions of the high priest or "Elder Brother" (*aḫu rabû*), who must rise at a prescribed time, ritually cleanse himself, recite specified prayers, and perform other ritual activities. The Elder Brother also orders and coordinates the work of others in the temple, including the "Temple Enterer" (*ērib-bīti*), the lamentation priests (*kalû*), singers (*nāru*), various craftsmen who produce objects required during the festival's rituals, and other temple staff. Most of these activities would pass unnoticed by the general populace.

The scope of the festival changes dramatically on the fifth day. In addition to the priests and temple staff, new actors enter the festival on this day. First, the statues of the patron gods of other cities are brought in through the city to the Esagila temple. Next, the king is brought to the temple, where he relinquishes his crown and other symbols of kingship to the high priest who then presents them to the statue of the god Marduk. The high priest then strikes the king on the cheek, pulls his ears, and makes him kneel before Marduk and recite a litany declaring that he has fulfilled his duties as king. In due course (the text is unfortunately damaged here, so the exact sequence of events is not fully clear), the high priest returns the crown and symbols of kingship to the king. The widening of the group of direct participants is also mirrored by an expansion of the location and visibility of cultic activities to outside of the temple complex. In particular, the procession of the statues of the gods and the arrival of the king at the temple would have been public events, visible to the general populace. Indeed, this would have been one of the few occasions when ordinary people would have seen either the statues of the gods or the king.

---

[8] For a detailed analysis of the festival, see Debourse (2022). A useful summary of the ritual activities is presented in Table 4 on pages 220–221 of that work.

Fig. 2: Obverse (a) and reverse (b) of MNB 1848, one of the sources for the Late Babylonian new year ritual. © 2007 Musée du Louvre / Raphaël Chipault. https://collections.louvre.fr/en/ark:/53355/cl010171664#.

Scheduled Time During the New Year Festival

The new year festival is by its very nature inextricably intertwined with time: the very occurrence of the festival is tied to the cycle of the calendar, and the festival's overall structure is governed by the passage of days. On each day of the festival, events are scheduled in two main ways: (i) specific moments of short time when ritual acts are to take place,[9] and (ii) actions to be performed once another action has been completed.[10]

---

9 The term "short time" refers to time at the sub-day level. For discussion of this concept, see, for example, Miller and Symons (2020).
10 For a listing of all references to time in the Late Babylonian new year festival texts, see Debourse (2022, 229).

Specified Moments of Time

The Babylonian day began at sunset with a period of night, sometimes referred to as "night of the xth" (GE₆ x), followed by the period of daylight, sometimes simply referred to as "the xth" (x or x.KAM). Two systems of short time were used by the Babylonians: a division of each of the night and daytime into three "watches" (EN.NUN), whose length varies with the seasons, and the use of fixed-length units of time called *bēru* and UŠ (30 UŠ = 1 *bēru*). The *bēru* and UŠ were always used to measure time intervals, either durations of some activity or the time interval between two events. Most often, one of these two events would be sunset or sunrise. As a consequence, there was no equivalent to our system of "hours o'clock" which exist independently of sunrise or sunset.[11]

Eight statements are found in the preserved new year festival texts which indicate the specific moment of time at which an action is to be performed. Three of these statements appear at the very beginning of the sections for days 2, 4, and 5. A partially preserved statement – the time indication is lost in the break in the text – is also found at the beginning of the section for day 3, which suggests that a similar statement began the entry for each day of the festival. These statements are formulaic and give a time during the night when the high priest should rise, bathe, and recite a particular prayer to Bēl. Only the time itself and the particular prayer changes between the days. I quote below the statement for day 2:

> [DIŠ] *ina* ITI.BÁR UD.2.KAM 1 DANNA GE₆ [ᵗᵘ́ᵍ]ŠEŠ.GAL ZI-*ma* A.MEŠ ÍD TU₅ [*ana*] IGI ᵈEN KU₄-*ma* ᵗᵘ́ᵍGALA.LAL *ina* IGI ᵈEN [*i*]-*de-ek-ku ana* ᵈEN ŠÙD.BI DUG₄.GA
>
> In Nisannu, the 2nd day, 1 *bēru* of night, the Elder Brother will rise and bathe (in) riverwater. He will enter [into] the presence of Bēl (i.e., Marduk) and remove the curtain in front of Bēl. He will recite the following prayer to Bēl:[12]

This introduction is followed by the words of the prayer. Of interest to us is the statement of the time at which the Elder Brother is instructed to rise and bathe. For the four days over which the texts describing the ritual are partially preserved we have the following entries:

Day 2: In Nisannu, the 2nd day, 1 *bēru* of night.
Day 3: In Nisannu, the 3rd day, [1 1/3 *bēru* of night].
Day 4: In Nisannu, the 4th day, 1 2/3 *bēru* of night.
Day 5: In Nisannu, the 5th day, 2 *bēru* of night.

---

11 On Babylonian systems of short time measurement, see Steele (2020).
12 DT 15 Obv. I 1–4; transliteration and translation adapted from Debourse (2022, 101).

Although the entry for day 3 is broken, it seems reasonable to reconstruct the time as above on the assumption that the number of *bēru* of night increases by 1/3 *bēru* each day.

Many scholars have interpreted the phrase "x *bēru* of night" (x DANNA GE$_6$) as the time before sunrise at which the priest should rise from his bed, with the priest rising successively earlier each night.[13] However, as already noted by Neugebauer and Sachs (1967, 213) and more recently by Debourse (2022, 230–231), this interpretation is certainly incorrect and the phrase refers to the time after sunset. In other scholarly texts, including astronomical texts which come from the same scholarly context, the time interval after sunset is usually indicated by the phrase GE$_6$ GIN (literally "night has gone") and the interval before sunrise by either GE$_6$ *ana* ZALÁG ("night (remaining) to dawn") or the abbreviated phrase *ana* ZALÁG ("(remaining) to dawn"). Some texts abbreviate the phrase indicating "after sunset", GE$_6$ GIN, simply to GE$_6$, which can be understood as meaning "night (has gone)" or perhaps "(into) the night." In any case, I know of no instances of GE$_6$ alone meaning "the time until sunrise" and GE$_6$ does not make sense as an abbreviation of GE$_6$ *ana* ZALÁG. There is no room for doubt, therefore, that the time that the priest should rise is given as a time after sunset and gets progressively later each night.

If we assume that the time that the priest must rise follows a linear progression, as is clearly the case for the preserved examples, we can reconstruct the time of rising for each day of the festival.[14] In particular, we find that the rising time on the first of the month, which is presumably the first day of the festival, would be at 2/3 *bēru* after sunset, and the priest would rise at sunrise, 6 *bēru* after sunset, on the 17th day.[15] Linear variations of this kind, where a time interval increases (or decreases) by a constant amount each day, are very common in what I term "schematic astronomy" in Babylonia.[16] This type of astronomy presents a fully self-con-

---

13 For this interpretation, see, for example, Bidmead (2002, 110) and Linssen (2004, 224).
14 For a list of the reconstructed times, which simply increase by 1/3 *bēru* per day, see Debourse (2022, 235).
15 Recall that a *bēru* corresponds to 2 hours, or one sixth of the length of night at the equinox. The Babylonian year begins in the spring around the time of the spring equinox. Traditional astronomical texts such as the compendium MUL.APIN place the spring equinox on the 15th of Nisannu. In practice, of course, the date of the equinox will change from year to year since the beginning of the month is determined by the appearance of the new moon crescent. During the Late Babylonian period, the beginning of year usually took place slightly after the date of the equinox. Nevertheless, the length of the night will be approximately 12 hours or 6 *bēru* during Nisannu.
16 For the term "schematic astronomy", see Steele (2017, 10–12). The most important text in the schematic astronomical tradition is the compendium MUL.APIN, which was composed sometime in the late second or early first millennium BCE and was widely copied, quoted, and its astronom-

sistent description of the celestial world through simple (if often, from our perspective, inaccurate) numerical schemes, centred around the so-called schematic year which comprises twelve 30-day months making a total of 360 days, a simplification of the actual Babylonian calendar with its 29- or 30-day months and twelve- or thirteen-month years. Within schematic astronomy, we find numerical functions which increase and decrease by constant amounts between a maximum and a minimum (known to modern scholars as "zigzag functions"). For example, the change in the length of night is represented by a zigzag function varying between 4 *bēru* at the winter solstice (assumed to be on the 15th of Month X) and 2 *bēru* at the summer solstice (the 15th of Month IV), with a mean value of 3 *bēru* at the solstices (the 15th of Month I and Month VII), and the duration of visibility of the moon during Month I varies from a minimum of zero on day 30 and a maximum of 3 *bēru* (i.e., all night) on day 15, with a daily change of 12 UŠ. Seen in this context, the variation in the time of rising of the priest over the days of the festival as presented in the new year festival texts seems also to be in this tradition of schematic modelling and, indeed, may well have been inspired by the tradition of schematic astronomy. This connection is perhaps unsurprising when we recall that the scholars responsible for the Late Babylonian new year festival texts were almost certainly some of the scholars writing astronomical texts.

The four other references to specific moments when actions are to be taken concern events during the day. Two of these passages use the standard formulation x DANNA ME NIM-*a* (literally "x *bēru* of day having risen") for the time after sunrise found in astronomical texts: MNB 1848 Obv. 38 states that at 1 *bēru* after sunrise, the Elder Brother will call for the exorcist to consecrate the temple and sprinkle water from wells associated with the Tigris and Euphrates on the temple, set up ritual drums, pass the censer through the temple, and so forth. Rev. IV 23–24 states that once he has completed all of this, at 1 2/3 *bēru* after sunrise (i.e., 2/3 *bēru* after he started this task), he is then to go out and call for the craftsmen and begin another sequence of ritual preparations and acts. BM 41577 Obv. III 23 states that after the Elder Brother has spoken a series of prayers (specified just before this), "at 1 *bēru* before sunset" (1 DANNA ME *ana* ŠÚ ^{d}UTU) he will enter into the presence of (the statue of) Bēl with his hands behind his back, stand in front of Bēl, and recite another prayer. Once more, the phrase 1 DANNA ME *ana* ŠÚ ^{d}UTU (literally "1 *bēru* of day to the setting of the sun") is identical to the standard formulation found in astronomical texts.

---

ical content further developed in the Late Babylonian period. For an edition, translation, and study of MUL.APIN, see Hunger and Steele (2019). For a discussion of the importance and use of MUL.APIN in the late period, see Steele (2021).

The final passage appears in BM 32485+ Rev. VI 13 and has caused some confusion among scholars. It reads:

e-nu-ma an-na-a i-pu-šú KI 20 ŠÚ 20 ˡúŠEŠ.GAL 40 GI.MEŠ GIŠ.MEŠ 3 KÙŠ.ÀM NU BAR.MEŠ NU ḪAŠ.MEŠ GIŠ.MEŠ *ma*-GAR (error for: GAR-*ma*) *rik-su ina e-ri* GIŠIMMAR *i-rak-ka-as-šú-nu-tú*

When he has done this, when it is 20 (UŠ) before sunset, the Elder Brother will arrange 40 reeds of 3 cubits (each), unpeeled, unbroken, straight and as a ritual arrangement he will tie them together with palm leaves.[17]

The passage continues with further ritual instructions for the Elder Brother. The confusion arises with the phrase KI 20 ŠÚ 20. The number 20 can also be read as a logogram for *šamáš* "the sun." Farber (1983, 216) took the first 20 to refer to the sun, the ŠÚ as a logogram for *irbû* "to set," and split the second 20 into a *u* attached as a phonetic complement to ŠÚ to indicate the long vowel at the end of *irbû* plus a second *u* which he assumed was a scribal error, and translated "when the sun sets."[18] Linssen (2004, 223) and Debourse (2022, 136) instead read the first 20 as U.U and understand this as the Akkadian word *šuššān* "one-third" and the second 20 to refer to the sun and interpret the phrase to refer to 1/3 *bēru* after sunset (note, the word *bēru* is not found in this passage, so in this interpretation its absence must be understood as a scribal error). However, as I have discussed above, times after sunset are always referred to by a variation of the phrase GE₆ GIN, which defines the time by the beginning of night rather than through reference to sunset (even though they are the same thing). Furthermore, taking 20 as *šuššān* "one-third" strikes me as a very contrived reading. The much simpler explanation is to take the first 20 as an unmarked (i. e., unitless) sexagesimal place-value number used to stand for 20 UŠ. This way of writing time intervals in UŠ comes out of the tradition of metrological tables and is very common in Late Babylonian astronomical texts.[19] The second 20 can then be read as *šamáš* and the phrase ŠÚ *šamáš* understood as either a scribal error for the standard terminology for "before sunset" *ana* ŠÚ *šamáš* (literally "to the setting of the sun") or as an abbreviation of that longer phrase.[20] This understanding is confirmed by the general struc-

---

[17] BM 32485 Rev. VI 13–16; transliteration and translation adapted from Debourse (2022, 133).
[18] Note that the addition of phonetic complements is optional in the writing of cuneiform. Thus, *irbû* can be written using the logogram ŠÚ alone or using the logogram plus phonetic compliment ŠÚ-*u*.
[19] See Steele (2020) for a discussion of this terminology for writing times with the unit UŠ (= 1/30 *bēru*).
[20] I suspect a simple scribal error: the sign *ana* is written with a single vertical wedge which could easily be skipped when copying. Note also the scribal error shortly after this where the scribe has written *ma*-GAR instead of GAR-*ma*.

ture of the ritual: this passage appears as part of the description of what happens during the day of the 5th of Nisannu. In Linssen's (2004, 223) and Debourse's (2022, 136) interpretation of 1/3 *bēru* after sunset, we would have moved on to the beginning of the 6th day of Nisannu. However, if that was the case, we would expect this passage to be preceded by the standard statement naming the new day and giving the time that the Elder Brother should rise and bathe.[21] It seems certain, therefore, that this passage refers to 20 UŠ before sunset.

Two observations can be made about the references to short time in the Late Babylonian new year festival texts. First, it is apparent that the terminology used to refer to short time is the same as that found in astronomical texts. This fact should not be surprising given that it seems almost certain that both types of texts were composed and copied by the same group of scribes in Babylon. As we know from other archival evidence, in particular from colophons naming the scribes copying texts, Late Babylonian scholarly activity was centred around the temple and the interests of these scholars branched out into many fields which had been considered more the preserve of disciplinary specialists in earlier periods. In particular, we see considerable evidence of the incorporation of astronomical and astrological concepts, terminology, and knowledge into a variety of ritual, medical, and other texts in this period.[22] Second, it is noticeable that all of the actions specified by timed moments concern the Elder Brother – in each case he and he alone must do something, even if this action might involve him instructing other temple employees in their actions. To some extent, this fact is not surprising given that the texts as a whole are centred around the Elder Brother's actions. Nevertheless, it seems significant that no other participants – human or divine – are instructed to do things at particular moments of time.

Sequential Events

The timing of some actions to be undertaken during the new year festival is indicated by reference to the completion of other actions. In particular, we find passages introduced by the terms "once" (in the sense of "once that such-and-such has been done") (TA for Akkadian *ultu*), "after" (EGIR for Akkadian *arki*), and "when" (*e-nu-ma*) another thing has happened. These three terms can be combined with each other and/or with the short time indications discussed in the previous

---

21 Furthermore, on day 6, the scheme for the rising of the Elder Brother would imply that he rises at 2 1/3 *bēru* after sunset. He would therefore still be asleep at 1/3 *bēru* after sunset.
22 See, for example, Geller (2014), Wee (2017), Krul (2019), Reynolds (2019), and Steele (2022).

section. At first sight, all three terms seem to refer to more or less the same thing: when one thing is finished, another should begin. But a closer examination of the way that they are used in the text, and in particular of what the preceding action was and who was performing it, suggests that there is a subtle difference between them and that an intentional choice was made as to which term was used in each case.

The term "once" (*ultu*) appears four times in the preserved new year festival texts: three times in more or less fully preserved passages and once in a fragmentary context.[23] In each of the three well-preserved cases, the passage refers to the Elder Brother having just completed reciting a prayer and prefaces him beginning another action. For example:

TA *naq-bit iq-bu-ú* ᵍⁱˢIG.MEŠ BAD-*te* ˡúKU₄.É.MEŠ *gab-bi* KU₄.MEŠ-*ma* ME-*šú-nu* GIM *šá* GÌ-*a* DÙ.MEŠ ˡúGALA.MEŠ *u* ˡúNAR.MEŠ KI.MIN

Once he has said the prayer, he will open the doors. All the temple-enterers will enter and they will perform their rites as usual. The lamentation priests and the singers, ditto.[24]

The term "after" (*arki*) appears only once in the preserved texts:

EGIR *ḫu-ub šá* É *e-nu-ma* 1 2/3 DANNA ME NIM-*a* ˡúŠEŠ.GAL É.UMUŠ.A È-*ma* DUMU.MEŠ ˡú*um-man-nu* DÙ.A.BI-*šú-nu* GÙ-*si*

After the consecration of the temple, when (at) 1 2/3 *bēru* after sunrise, the Elder Brother of Eumuša will go out and call for all the craftsmen.[25]

The text specifies that the act of consecrating the temple is mostly to be carried out by the exorcist and the slaughterer who, when they have completed their work, are sent out of the city until the twelfth day of the festival. Indeed, it is stated that the Elder Brother may not see the consecration of the temple. Thus, "after" here refers to an action undertaken by individuals other than the Elder Brother. He has no direct control over how long it takes. The text therefore uses the more ambiguous term "after" rather than the consequential expression "once" to indicate that the Elder Brother's next act should occur following the completion of the consecration of the temple but not necessarily immediately following it. Instead, as the text goes on, it should be performed at 1 2/3 *bēru* after sunrise, by which time the temple's consecration should have been completed.

---

23 Well-preserved cases: DT 15 Obv. I 36, MNB 1848 Obv. III 34, and BM 41577 Obv. III 22. Fragmentary case: DT 15 Obv. II 8.
24 MNB 1848 Obv. III 34–37; transliteration and translation adapted from Debourse (2022, 149).
25 MNB 1848 Rev. IV 23–25; transliteration and translation adapted from Debourse (2022, 151).

The term "when" (*enūma*) appears most often and seems to have the most general meaning.[26] It can appear before statements of a specific short time (e.g., "when (at) 1 2/3 *bēru* after sunrise"[27]), or be used for simple sequences of actions (e.g., "when he has done this"[28]), and is sometimes combined with either "once" or "after" statements. Unlike "once," which seems to only be used for sequences of actions where both are performed by the Elder Brother, or "after," which is used for a sequence where the first action was ordered by the Elder Brother but performed by someone else, "when" seems to be used for a wider variety of triggering actions, including the arrival of the statue of the god Nabu at the temple over which the Elder Brother had no direct control.[29]

It appears, therefore, that we have three types of sequential time in the new year festival texts: actions to be performed by the Elder Brother which occur immediately "once" another action by him has been completed, marking a change in his actions within a continuous ritual act; actions to be performed by the Elder Brother at some time "after" the completion of an action ordered by him but performed by someone else directly connected with the temple; and actions to be performed by the Elder Brother "when" something else has happened, this something else being an action by either the Elder Brother or by someone else, including individuals not part of the temple staff, such as the king and the divine statues, or, alternatively, "when" a specific moment of short time has been reached. "When," therefore, is used for actions made in response to an external trigger, outside of the direct control of the Elder Brother either because they are performed by other actors or because they are governed by astronomically defined moments of time.

Experiencing Time During the New Year Festival

As I have discussed in the preceding section, the Late Babylonian new year festival texts provide detailed information of how time is scheduled during the festival. But, as we would expect of Babylonian ritual texts, which are typically prescriptive of how the ritual should be performed rather than descriptive of how it was performed, they do not discuss how time was experienced by the various participants during the festival. We can perhaps gain a few hints from passages in these texts

---

26 Interestingly, as Debourse (2022, 191) has highlighted, by the Late Babylonian period, the previously fairly common term *enūma* had more or less dropped out of use, with the exception of within ritual contexts.
27 MNB 1848 Rev. IV 23–24: *e-nu-ma 1 2/3 DANNA ME NIM-a*.
28 BM 32485+DT 109 Rev. VI 13 and MNB 1848 Obv. II 21: *e-nu-ma an-na-a i-te-ep-šú*.
29 MNB Rev. IV 24–25.

which state, for example, that after completing their work consecrating the temple, the exorcist and the slaughterer will leave the city and wait in the hinterland from the fifth to the twelfth day; one can imagine that time might drag for these individuals as compared to those actively participating in the rest of the festival. But beyond that the new year festival texts themselves provide little evidence.

It is generally assumed that certain parts of the new year festival were celebrated publicly and widely within the city. For example, the procession of the king and of the divine statues through the streets to the temple would likely be one of the few times – perhaps the only time – during the year that the general population could catch a glimpse of them, and indirect evidence from (much) earlier periods suggests that the festival was a time of celebration, with abundant food and drink, and crowd-lined streets.[30] It has even been suggested that the fourth, eighth, and eleventh days of the festival were public holidays.[31] If correct, this assumption would suggest a significant difference in the experience of time between those days and the other days of the festival when the rituals were performed wholly within the temple and its environs by priests and other temple employees without a public audience. However, these claims are based upon much earlier evidence and, as convincingly argued by Debourse (2022), we have little evidence to suggest that the new year festival was actually performed in the late period, or if it was, then it was on a significantly reduced scale to earlier times. The historical sections of the Babylonian Astronomical Diaries from this period, for example, do not seem to refer to the new year festival, despite noting the celebration of several other festivals.

Indeed, whether or not the festival was performed in the Late Babylonian period, it is apparent that many activities in the city continued uninterrupted during the time at which the festival would take place. Business and other legal transactions, for example, seem to have continued as normal during the festival. This conclusion can be shown directly for the Neo-Babylonian period (slightly earlier than the Late Babylonian texts we have been looking at) by simply counting the number of texts dated to the different days of the month. A search of the open access PROSOBAB (Prosopography of Babylonia, c. 620–330 BCE) database compiled at Leiden University,[32] which currently (October 2022) contains entries from 5127 tablets, yields between four and sixteen texts written on each of the first fifteen days of Nisannu. Nine, eight, and five tablets are dated to days four, eight, and eleven of Nisannu, which van der Toorn argues were public holidays; these numbers are

---

30 Bidmead (2002, 4 and 13–14).
31 Van der Toorn (1991, 334).
32 See https://prosobab.leidenuniv.nl [last access 23/11/2023].

very similar to the numbers of tablets written on the same days of the second month (respectively eleven, seven, and seven), suggesting that there was no holiday from business on those days. Astronomical texts tell a similar story: astronomical observations continued to be made on each day of the festival, without interruption. Given that the scholars who made these observations and wrote these texts were closely associated with the temple, often holding temple positions, this lack of interruption of astronomical observation implies at the very least that the temple was not closed to normal business during the new year festival.

It seems, therefore, either that the new year festival had ceased to be performed by the Late Babylonian period, or that its performance was considerably slimmed down, with little role for the general population or even most of the temple staff. Given this conclusion, we can say very little about how time was experienced during the new year festival.

Final Remarks

The Late Babylonian new year festival texts attest to several connections between time and the festival. In addition to the regular role of the calendar in providing an overall framework for the festival, we find considerable evidence for both short time indications triggering the commencement of ritual actions and the use of sequential language to mark the transition between ritual acts and to coordinate the activities of the Elder Brother and other participants in the festival. The short time indications use systems of time measurement that are most widely known from astronomical texts, and which are, in effect, defined by astronomical phenomena, namely sunrise and sunset. Indeed, the terminology used to indicate these moments of short time directly parallels what we find in contemporary astronomical texts. Although this use of shared terminology is not surprising given that the two types of texts were written by the same group of scribes, it reflects a change from earlier ritual texts which rarely include short time indications.[33] As Krul has suggested, there seems to be an increased astralization of rituals in the late period, with other late ritual texts giving a role to certain stars, constellations, and planets within the ritual, either as the objects of prayers or as observed phenomena which can trigger ritual acts.[34] The new year ritual texts support this conclusion.

---

33 Steele (2020, 104–107).
34 Krul (2019).

References

Bidmead, Julye. 2002. *The Akītu Festival. Religious Continuity and Royal Legitimation in Mesopotamia.* Piscataway: Gorgias.

Debourse, Céline. 2022. *Of Priests and Kings: The Babylonian New Year Festival in the Last Age of Cuneiform Culture.* Leiden: Brill.

Falassi, Alessandro. 1967. *Time out of Time: Essays on the Festival.* Albuquerque: University of New Mexico Press.

Farber, Walter. 1983. "Kultische Rituale." In *Texte aus der Umwelt des Alten Testaments. Bd. II: Orakel, Rituale, Bau- und Votivinschriften, Lieder und Gebete*, edited by Otto Kaiser, 212–234. Gütersloh: G. Mohr.

Geller, Markham J. 2014. *Melothesia in Babylonia: Medicine, Magic, and Astrology in the Ancient Near East.* Berlin: De Gruyter.

Hunger, Hermann, and John Steele. 2019. *The Babylonian Astronomical Compendium MUL.APIN.* Abingdon: Routledge.

Krul, Julia. 2019. "Star Anu, Lord of Heaven: The Influence of the Celestial Sciences on Temple Rituals in Hellenistic Uruk and Babylon." In *Scholars and Scholarship in Late Babylonian Uruk*, edited by Christine Proust and John Steele, 219–234. New York: Springer.

Linssen, Marc J. H. 2004. *The Cults of Uruk and Babylon. The Temple Ritual Texts as Evidence for Hellenistic Cult Practice.* Leiden: Brill.

Miller, Kassandra J., and Sarah L. Symons. 2020. "Introduction." In *Down to the Hour: Short Time in the Ancient Mediterranean and Near East*, edited by Kassandra J. Miller and Sarah L. Symons, 1–13. Leiden: Brill.

Neugebauer, Otto, and Abraham Sachs. 1967. "Some Atypical Astronomical Cuneiform Texts I." *Journal of Cuneiform Studies* 21:183–218.

Pallis, Svend Aage. 1926. *The Babylonian Akitu Festival.* Copenhagen: Andr. Fred. Høst & Søn.

Pongratz-Leisten, Beate. 1994. *Ina Šulmi Īrub. Die kulttopographische und ideologische Programmatik der akītu-Prozession in Babylonien und Assyrien im I. Jahrtausend v. Chr.* Mainz: Philipp von Zabern.

Reynolds, Frances. 2019. *A Babylon Calendar Treatise: Scholars and Invaders in the Late First Millennium BC.* Oxford: Oxford University Press.

Steele, John. 2017. *Rising Time Schemes in Babylonian Astronomy.* New York: Springer.

Steele, John. 2020. "Short Time in Mesopotamia." In *Down to the Hour: Short Time in the Ancient Mediterranean and Near East*, edited by Kassandra J. Miller and Sarah L. Symons, 90–124. Leiden: Brill.

Steele, John. 2021. "The Continued Relevance of MUL.APIN in Late Babylonian Astronomy." *Journal of Ancient Near Eastern History* 8:259–277.

van der Toorn, Karel. 1991. "The Babylonian New Year Festival: New Insights from the Cuneiform Texts and their Bearing on Old Testament Study." In *Congress Volume Leuven 1989*, edited by J. A. Emberton, 331–344. Leiden: Brill.

Wee, John Z. 2017. "Pan-astronomical Hermeneutics and the Arts of the Lamentation Priest." *Zeitschrift für Assyriologie* 107:236–260.

Glenn W. Most
"The Tragic Day"

At a critical moment of Aristophanes' comedy *Thesmophoriazusae* (*The Women Celebrating the Thesmophoria*), Euripides, who is a character in the play, expresses acute dread lest the assembly of women condemn him to death. He cries out in terror, ὦ Ζεῦ, τί δρᾶσαι διανοεῖ με **τήμερον**; ("O Zeus, what do you mean to do to me **today?**" 71).[1] And only a few lines later, he returns to the subject of this day to proclaim, τῇδε θἠμέρᾳ κριθήσεται | εἴτ' ἔστ' ἔτι ζῶν εἴτ' ἀπόλωλ' Εὑριπίδης ("**This very day** it will be adjudged: does Euripides live on, or is he a goner?" 76–77). Then immediately afterwards he goes on once again to explain his situation: αἱ γὰρ γυναῖκες ἐπιβεβουλεύκασί μοι | κἀν Θεσμοφόροιν μέλλουσι περί μου **τήμερον** | ἐκκλησιάζειν ἐπ' ὀλέθρῳ ("The women, you see, have devised a plot against me, and **today** in the sanctuary of the Two Thesmophoroi they're going to hold an assembly on the question of my destruction." 82–84). And a hundred lines later he returns yet again to the same topic: μέλλουσί μ' αἱ γυναῖκες ἀπολεῖν **τήμερον** | τοῖς Θεσμοφορίοις, ὅτι κακῶς αὐτὰς λέγω ("The women at the Thesmophoria are preparing to destroy me **this very day**, because I slander them." 181–182).

Obviously, Euripides is extremely worried about what might happen to him, and not about what might happen to him some day in the imaginable future, but in particular about what seems likely to be about to happen to him on the very same day during the course of which we happen to encounter him expressing this worry. His repeated references to that specific day are made all the more emphatic by being placed conspicuously in every instance, either at the beginning of the sentence or at the end of the line. These references are manifestly not random or insignificant: they are indicating what is for Euripides a crucial part of the perilous situation in which he finds himself. He is in mortal danger: and what is more, today is the very day on which that danger is coming to a head. Not only is this danger associated with this day: the two seem to be inextricably and essentially linked with one another.

This comic episode featuring the tragic poet Euripides belongs to what are called the "paratragic" scenes of ancient Greek comedies – that is, scenes that parody the conventions and language of the ancient Greek tragedies that were staged in the same years, and sometimes in the very same theaters and festivals and usu-

---

1 Greek texts and English translations of this play are taken from Henderson (2014).

ally before the very same audiences, as the comedies were.[2] These scenes, which occur with some frequency in the plays of Old Comedy, provide one convenient way to find out how ordinary audiences in ancient Athens understood the tragedies that they regularly watched in their theaters, for the comic poets were hoping to raise a laugh by caricaturing aspects of tragedies that their own audiences would find immediately recognizable as characteristic of tragedy.[3] Such aspects were not funny in the tragedies themselves – indeed, they could contribute powerfully to the tragic effects that convulsed and enthralled spectators. But once they were taken out of the context of the tragedies in which they had been so effective and were inserted instead into the alien and ludicrous framework of comedies, they could suddenly reveal themselves to be bizarre and hence potentially risible phenomena. That is, the laughter of the comic poet, and that of the comic audience, could serve metatheatrically to thematize the literary, unrealistic character of the tragic conventions and thereby to unmask them as being fundamentally "funny," in both senses of the English word: as being peculiar or odd, and thereby as inciting laughter.

If Aristophanes' Euripides had only referred once to this fateful day, his words might have been overlooked or discounted. But as it is, his references are repeated and conspicuous. So this gag surely suggests that Aristophanes and his viewers were able to recognize references to that day as being especially typical of tragedy – that is, that it was especially characteristic of tragedies to focus the spectators' attention upon that single and particular day on which the tragic crisis either seemed to be about to happen or else was indeed in the very course of happening. This day we can call "the tragic day." It is the one day that is selected by tragedy out of all the thousands of days that make up this month and this year and all the years of time, as the only day on which the tragic catastrophe can happen, must happen, and therefore inevitably will happen. Euripides was a celebrated and controversial tragic poet; in Aristophanes' comedy he suddenly discovers that he is a tragic character in his very own tragedy, not one that he has composed but one in which he is himself the mortally endangered protagonist. He suddenly realizes that the tragic day is not only a literary trope, but also, for him, in this comic fantasy, a life-threatening experience.

In his *Poetics*, Aristotle discusses a different but closely related aspect of the tragic day. Comparing tragedy with epic, he writes,

---

[2] The basic treatment remains Rau (1967).
[3] For another example of the use of comic paratragedy to identify an element ancient Greek audiences would have recognized as being typical of tragedy, cf. Most (2013).

ἡ μὲν οὖν ἐποποιία τῇ τραγῳδίᾳ μέχρι μὲν τοῦ μετὰ μέτρου λόγῳ μίμησις εἶναι σπουδαίων ἠκολούθησεν· τῷ δὲ τὸ μέτρον ἁπλοῦν ἔχειν καὶ ἀπαγγελίαν εἶναι, ταύτῃ διαφέρουσιν· ἔτι δὲ τῷ μήκει· ἡ μὲν ὅτι μάλιστα πειρᾶται ὑπὸ **μίαν περίοδον ἡλίου** εἶναι ἢ μικρὸν ἐξαλλάττειν, ἡ δὲ ἐποποιία ἀόριστος τῷ χρόνῳ καὶ τούτῳ διαφέρει, καίτοι τὸ πρῶτον ὁμοίως ἐν ταῖς τραγῳδίαις τοῦτο ἐποίουν καὶ ἐν τοῖς ἔπεσιν.

Epic matches tragedy to the extent of being mimesis of elevated matters in metrical language; but they differ in that epic has an unchanging metre and is in narrative mode. They also differ in length: tragedy tends so far as possible to stay within **a single revolution of the sun**, or close to it, while epic is unlimited in time span and is distinctive in this respect (though to begin with the poets followed this same practice in tragedy as in epic). (*Poetics* 5 1449b12–16)[4]

Aristotle's point is somewhat different from Euripides' in the *Thesmophoriazusae*. Euripides' concern with the tragic day is focused on the menace that *this one present day*, in contrast to any other day, offers to his very survival. His worry is that this will be his last day, that the whole future length of his life will be one day or even less. Aristotle, instead, is thinking about the length of a day, and is arguing that tragedy, unlike epic, tries to limit its action to the duration of *a single day*, whatever day that might happen to be. For Euripides, the day, by reason of its presentness, confronts him with a terrifying threat in its immediacy and urgency. For Aristotle, what matters is that the duration of a single day is long enough to encompass a whole action – evidently, he is presupposing here the concept of a single, unified action as comprising a beginning, a middle, and an end, which he elaborates a few pages later (*Poetics* 7 1450b23–34). And yet these two understandings of the tragic day are clearly connected with one another. What makes the tragic day tragic for Euripides is his dread that the misfortune it contains, and indeed his life in its entirety, will conclude as a whole once and for all before the end of that same day. Thus both his conception and Aristotle's revolve centrally around the postulated finality of a completed tragic event: the difference is that Euripides emphasizes its urgent proximity, Aristotle its limited duration.

Aristotle's claim that tragedy "tends so far as possible" to confine itself to a single revolution of the sun, "or close to it," was most likely not intended as a prescriptive rule to which he was requiring future poets of tragedy to adhere as far as possible – though precisely this was how this sentence tended to be understood by the French and Italian Neoclassical theoreticians of tragedy, who partly based upon it their demand that tragedians obey the three unities of time, place, and action.[5] Instead, it seems to be descriptive and to be indicating a general tendency

---

4 The Greek text and English translations of this treatise are taken from Halliwell, Fyfe, Innes (1995).
5 E.g., Robortello (1968, 50).

which was not always respected but which underwent a historical development towards greater restrictiveness in this regard.

In fact, this description, so understood, is confirmed by most of the surviving Greek tragedies: by far the greater number of these contain an action that takes place from beginning to end within the compass of a single day.[6] Indeed, some tragedies indicate explicitly that the start of the play's action coincides with daybreak: thus the prologue of Aeschylus' *Agamemnon* takes place in the last hours of the night before daybreak, as the watchman's first speech, invoking the stars of the nightly heavens, makes clear (1–19); but we can be certain that the day has begun by line 508, when the messenger greets the risen sun.

In the tragedies that were composed by the real tragic poet Euripides (as distinguished from the fictional tragic poet Euripides who is a character in several of Aristophanes' comedies), it occasionally happens that, after the catastrophe, someone points out how lamentable the day that all have just experienced has been: so for example the Nurse in the *Andromache* exclaims, "My dear ladies, how disaster follows upon disaster **this day** (ἐν τῇδ᾽ ἡμέρᾳ 803)!" 802–803).[7] But even more characteristic of Euripides' tragedies are prologues in which the speaker foreshadows the events to come by announcing that the day on which the action is going to take place will be decisive – surely Euripides favors this device because in this way the audience are put into a state of anxious anticipation and suspense. The conspicuous placement of these announcements at the very beginning of the plays in question must have struck spectators as being typical of Euripides: in this regard, Aristophanes' caricature is quite accurate. Thus at the beginning of the *Alcestis* Apollo says about the heroine, "She is now on the point of death, held up by the arms of her family within the house, for it is **on this day** (τῇδε [...] ἐν ἡμέρᾳ 20) that she is fated to die" (19–21), and he adds a few lines later, when he sees Death approaching for her, "He has arrived punctually, watching for **today** (τόδ᾽ ἦμαρ 27) when she must die." (24–27) So too, in the opening of the *Hippolytus*, Aphrodite, enraged with Hippolytus, declares, "Yet for his sins against me I shall **this day** (ἐν τῇδ᾽ ἡμέρᾳ 22) punish Hippolytus. I have long since come far with my plans, and I need little further effort." (21–23) In the prologue of *Hecuba*, Polydorus says of Polyxena, "For fate is leading my sister to her death **on this day** (τῷδ᾽ [...] ἐν ἤματι 44)." (43–44) And Electra announces at the beginning of the *Orestes* the fate that on that very day impends for Orestes and herself:

> Argos has decreed that no one is to receive us under his roof or at his fireside or even speak to us since we are matricides. And **this is the appointed day** (κυρία δ᾽ ἥδ᾽ ἡμέρα 48) on which

---

6 Schwindt (1994).
7 Greek texts and English translations of Euripides are taken from Kovacs (1994–2002).

the city will vote whether we two must die by stoning [or someone must whet a sword and thrust it upon our necks]. (46–51)

It is noteworthy that in most of these examples the day in question has not been chosen at random but has been assigned by fate – and by the same token, the event that is scheduled to transpire on that day cannot be postponed or annulled by any merely human agency but is instead just as fixed and inalterable as the destiny that has imposed it. Moreover, the event that will happen on this day is generally not just any everyday occurrence, but the most important occurrence of all: an impending death, and not that of just anyone, but rather the death of one of the principal characters of the play. The tragic day is tragic not only because it is typical of tragedy, but also because it is involved in a circumstance that is peculiarly characteristic of tragedies: death.

Euripides' *Medea* makes a particularly novel and interesting use of this topic of the tragic day. Medea has been banished from Corinth by King Creon, who fears what she might do to him and to those he loves if she remains in the city. But she manages to persuade him to give her a respite of a single day so that she can put her affairs into order:

> Allow me to remain **this one day** (μίαν [...] τήνδ᾽ [...] ἡμέραν 340) and to complete my plans for exile and how I may provide for my children, since their father does not care to do so. (340–343)

She appeals to his most humane sentiments, his pity and his sense of guilt for his involvement in Jason's mistreatment of her. Creon accedes to this request – after all, he might wonder, quite reasonably, what harm could she possibly do him in a single day? But his sympathy with her is not unlimited: he warns her, "if **tomorrow's sun** (ἡ 'πιοῦσα λαμπὰς [...] θεοῦ 352) sees you and your children within the borders of this land, you will be put to death." (352–354)

And yet as it will turn out, by granting her this concession at the same time he is signing the warrant of his and his daughter's death. As soon as he leaves the stage, Medea gloats:

> But he has reached such a pitch of folly that, while it lay in his power to check my plans by banishing me, he has permitted me to stay **for this day** (τήνδ᾽ [...] ἡμέραν 373), a day on which I shall make corpses of three of my enemies, the father, his daughter, and my husband. (371–375)

Creon was a victim of the illusion that this present day was a day just like any other one, a day which he could grant as an apparently harmless respite to Medea without changing his own situation in the least. This might have been the case had Creon been living in the ordinary world; what he has failed to realize is that in fact he is a character in a tragedy, and that his perfectly understandable but in fact catastrophic decision to give Medea a grace period for a single day will transform that day from an ordinary one into a tragic day. His free but blind decision to ease Medea's situation slightly for a single day was sufficient to plunge him and his whole household into irremediable disaster.

In Sophocles too the tragic day recurs often, though perhaps somewhat less mechanically and predictably than it does in Euripides. In *Oedipus the King*, Teiresias' altercation with Oedipus climaxes in the seer's predicting enigmatically, "**This day** (ἥδ' ἡμέρα) shall be your parent and your destroyer." (438)[8] And after the catastrophe has been revealed to all, the Second Messenger comments on what has happened in words that echo and explain Teiresias' prediction:

> These horrors burst forth not from one person, but brought commingled grief to man and woman. Their earlier happiness was truly happiness; but now in **this day** (τῇδε θἠμέρα 1283) lamentation, ruin, death, shame, all ills that can be named, none of them is absent. (1280–1285)

In *The Trachinian Women*, once Hyllus has seen Heracles begin to suffer the mortal torments that Deianeira's poisoned gift inflicts upon him, the son bitterly accuses his mother, "Know that on **this day** (τῇδ' ἐν ἡμέρᾳ 740) you have killed your husband – yes, my father!" (739–740)

In most of the Sophoclean examples, the tragic day is not announced from the very beginning, as it is in Euripides; instead, the terminology tends to be applied retrospectively to events only once their full catastrophic dimensions have become unmistakably clear. Teiresias is the sole character who is privy to the kind of superhuman knowledge that would permit him, like many Euripidean characters, to forecast the coming tragedy as being inevitable; Sophocles' characters tend instead to be imprisoned within an insuperably limited degree of merely human knowledge and hence they are capable of recognizing their true predicament only later, much too late.

The *Ajax* provides a partial exception that in the end confirms this rule. It turns out late in this play that Athena is furious at Ajax and will ensure his death, but that this can happen exclusively on this one day. Ultimately this knowledge derives from the seer Calchas; but it is transmitted only by an anonymous human messenger, who warns that Ajax must be kept indoors for that one day if he is to survive it:

---

8 Greek texts and English translations of Sophocles are taken from Lloyd-Jones (1994).

So much as this I know, since I was there. Calchas moved away on his own from the group assembled around the commanders, apart from the sons of Atreus, placed his hand in Teucer's in friendly fashion, and spoke, charging him by every means to keep Ajax in the hut during **this present day** (κατ' ἦμαρ τοὐμφανὲς τὸ νῦν τόδε 753) and not to let him out, if he wished ever to see him alive. For the anger of divine Athena shall pursue him **for this day only** (τήνδ' [...] ἡμέραν μόνην 756), so Calchas said. (748–757)

Why Athena's anger has such a short effective duration, and why she would not be capable of destroying Ajax even if he remained within his hut, are questions that the play does not pause to answer, or even to pose. Instead, the messenger repeats over and over again the urgency of the danger posed by this one day: "By such words as these he brought on himself the unappeasable anger of the goddess, through his more than mortal pride. But if he is still alive **this day** (τῇδ' [...] ἡμέρᾳ 778), perhaps with a god's help we may preserve him." (776–779); Tecmessa: "Ah me, from what man did he learn this?" Messenger: "From the prophet who is son of Thestor, a word that on **this day** (καθ' ἡμέραν | τὴν νῦν 801–802) brings death or life for him." (800–802) But of course this news comes much too late to be of any use: for by the time we hear these words, Ajax has already left the hut and gone out to the place where in the very next episode he will kill himself. Here alone in these examples from Sophocles can humans attain some degree of a superhuman level of knowledge – but they can do so only indirectly and futilely, for by the time the divine message reaches them it is far too late for them to be able to apply it in such a way as to prevent the tragic outcome.

How is this tragic focus on the tragic day to be explained? The question has been much discussed in the history of the study of Greek tragedy, and various possible answers have been proposed, among them the following:

– *Focalization of attention and intensification of dramatic suspense.* As Aristotle suggests, one of the ways in which tragedy is superior to epic is its greater restriction of the temporal duration of its action:

> ἔτι τῷ ἐν ἐλάττονι μήκει τὸ τέλος τῆς μιμήσεως εἶναι (τὸ γὰρ ἀθροώτερον ἥδιον ἢ πολλῷ κεκραμένον τῷ χρόνῳ, λέγω δ' οἷον εἴ τις τὸν Οἰδίπουν θείη τὸν Σοφοκλέους ἐν ἔπεσιν ὅσοις ἡ Ἰλιάς).
>
> Also, tragedy excels by achieving the goal of its mimesis in a shorter scope; greater concentration is more pleasurable than dilution over a long period: suppose someone were to arrange Sophocles' *Oedipus* in as many hexameters as the *Iliad*. (*Poetics* 26 1462b1–3)

By concentrating all the action into the brief compass of a single day, the tragic poet heightens the urgency of his plot and increases the suspense felt by the characters, chorus, and presumably audience. We might describe this as a *psychological* or *psychagogical* explanation.

- *Ephemerality as the fundamental condition of human existence.* It is a commonplace of early Greek thought that humans, unlike gods, do not enjoy a stable condition but that their whole life can be changed entirely by the events of a single day; this radical inconstancy is referred to by Pindar and other poets as human ephemerality.[9] This is what Athena is indicating at the beginning of Sophocles' *Ajax* when she draws the lesson from Ajax's downfall and says to Odysseus,

> Look, then, at such things, and never yourself utter an arrogant word against the gods, nor assume conceit because you outweigh another in strength or in profusion of great wealth. Know that **a single day** (ἡμέρα 131) brings down or raises up again all mortal things, and the gods love those who think sensibly and detest offenders! (127–133)

So too, the Nurse in the same poet's *Trachinian Women* interprets the downfall of Deianeira in the same moral terms: "That is how things stand here; so that if anyone reckons on **two days or more** (δύο | ἢ κἀπὶ πλείους ἡμέρας 943–944), he is acting foolishly, for there is no **tomorrow** (αὔριον 945) till one has got through **today** (τὴν παροῦσαν ἡμέραν 946) in happiness." (943–947) By limiting his dramatic action to a single day, the tragic poet reminds his human spectators of the fact that they cannot count on their current condition as lasting any longer than that. This explanation, by contrast with the first one, is *anthropological* and *ontological*.

- *The continuous presence of the chorus.* Lessing proposed a concrete *dramaturgical* or *technical* explanation for this concentration of tragedy on a single action in a single time and place:

> Die Einheit der Handlung war das erste dramatische Gesetz der Alten; die Einheit der Zeit und die Einheit des Ortes waren gleichsam nur Folgen aus jener, die sie schwerlich strenger beobachtet haben würden, als es jene notwendig erfordert hätte, wenn nicht die Verbindung des Chors dazu gekommen wäre. Da nämlich ihre Handlungen eine Menge Volks zum Zeugen haben mussten und diese Menge immer die nämliche blieb, welche sich weder weiter von ihren Wohnungen entfernen, noch länger aus denselben wegbleiben konnte, als man gewöhnlichermassen der blossen Neugierde wegen zu tun pflegt: so konnten sie fast nicht anders, als den Ort auf einen und ebendenselben individuellen Platz, und die Zeit auf **einen und ebendenselben Tag** einschränken.
>
> Unity of action was the first dramatic law among the ancients; the unity of time and unity of place were both only consequences of that first law, which they would not have observed as more than absolutely necessary had the incorporation of the chorus not been added. But because their actions required a crowd of people as witnesses, and because this crowd always remained the same and could neither distance themselves from their homes nor remain outside longer than one normally would out of mere curiosity, the ancients could hardly do oth-

---

9 The classic discussion remains Fränkel (1946).

erwise than to limit the location to a single individual spot and the time to **one single day**. (G. E. Lessing, *Hamburgische Dramaturgie*, 46. Stück)

Given that the chorus in a Greek tragedy arrives on the scene near the very beginning of the play and remains present there until the very end, what are they to do if during the action the sun sets? Where do they sleep? Do they just lie down on the ground? Or do they go home? Obviously, this dilemma could pose considerable embarrassment for the staging of a play, and one way to avoid it is to keep the action within the limits of a single day. And yet there are tragedies in which the action takes place in two different locales – most notably Aeschylus' *Eumenides* and Sophocles' *Ajax* – and in these cases the chorus leaves the scene from the first locale and reenters it in the second one; so perhaps this dramaturgical difficulty would not have been insuperable if the tragedians insisted upon having a play whose action extended beyond a single day.

There is no reason to think that any one of these proposed explanations, or any other one, is the single necessary and sufficient answer that can resolve this conundrum. Instead, it seems likelier that each such proposal illuminates a different aspect of a particularly complicated phenomenon. Perhaps, in this spirit, one might add a further suggestion to the pile:

– *The festival days, the ones on which the Greater Dionysian festival was celebrated.* The Greek tragedies were staged at the Greater Dionysian festival, presumably as an offering to the god Dionysus. Every year, the festival took place from the 10th to the 16th days of the Attic month of Elaphebolion: five days all in all were set aside for the celebrations, including performances of tragedies on three days, of comedies on one, and of dithyrambs on one; it is known that the performances began at dawn on each of these days but it is not certain which days exactly were the ones dedicated to which of these performances.[10] This meant that all year long, the audiences knew that starting at sunrise on a certain day tragedies would be performed, and that hence on that one day the fates of the characters whose vicissitudes were the subject of these tragedies would be decided, so that it would be determined whether they would survive or be destroyed. In this sense, the tragic day would be the day on which a tragedy was performed. This would be a *religious* or *institutional* explanation.

What dates these performances would have corresponded to in our own calendar is difficult to determine, given that the Attic calendar was lunisolar and that the dates shifted from year to year. But what is certain is that the lunar month Elaphe-

---

10 Mikalson (1975, 125–130, 137, 201); Pickard-Cambridge (1968, 57–83).

bolion straddled the vernal equinox, i.e., that it corresponded roughly to March-April in our solar calendar, and that Elaphebolion 10–16 were the days right in the middle of that month. Thucydides for example writes that the treaty that established the Peace of Nicias was made "as the winter was ending, in the spring, immediately after the city Dionysia." (5.20.1) Hence there is a good chance that at least in some years the Attic tragedies were performed exactly on or at least very close to the vernal equinox around 20 March.

Perhaps then we can suggest a further possible explanatory hypothesis, a *symbolic* one:

– For might we not regard the tragic day as a demonization of the festival day on which the tragedies were produced? To be sure, it is one of the laws of Greek tragedy that, unlike comedies, tragedies never make explicit reference to the actual conditions of stage production but only do so implicitly and only if such references can be understood within the fictional world of the play. So the tragic day is the day that the tragic characters experience as being tragic; but it is also the festival day that is experienced by the theater audience as being tragic, albeit in a different sense. The audience's knowledge that the tragedy was to be performed on a certain day is introjected into the minds of the characters within the tragedy themselves, where, given the terrible events that await them, it takes on a deadly, demonic urgency. For the audience, the tragic day is a matter of the calendar; for the characters, it is a question of life or death.

And perhaps there is even more. For the vernal equinox is one of the two days of the year on which day and night are balanced equally on the razor's edge. Starting the very next day, every day will become longer, and every night shorter. But the equinox itself is the day of crisis. Will the tragic characters survive it or not? Will they live on to see the days becoming ever longer, or will they be overwhelmed by night? They do not yet know; and the audience is there to find out what will happen.[11]

What a remarkable way the Athenians invented to celebrate the beginning of spring: to remind themselves of the precariousness of the human condition and of the likelihood of disaster and grief. How Greek!

---

11 And perhaps we might finally suggest a *poetological* hypothesis. For what is at stake in the tragic day is not only the tragic character's own life or death, but also the success or failure of the tragedy which the tragic poet has composed and which is set into a competition with two other poets' productions. Only one of them can be proclaimed the victor; only one can have his name inscribed as victorious on the victory lists; only one can achieve the only kind of immortality that a human poet can hope for.

References

Fränkel, Hermann. 1946. "Man's 'Ephemeros' Nature according to Pindar and Others." *TAPhA* 77:131–145.

Halliwell, Stephen, Fyfe, W. H., and Doreen C. Innes. 1995. *Aristotle. Poetics* (ed. and transl. S. Halliwell), *Longinus. On the Sublime* (trans. W. H. Fyfe, rev. Donald H. Russell), *Demetrius. On Style* (ed. and trans. Doreen C. Innes). Loeb Classical Library 199. Cambridge MA: Harvard University Press.

Henderson, Jeffrey. 2014. *Aristophanes. Birds, Lysistrata, Women at the Thesmophoria*. Loeb Classical Library 179. Cambridge MA: Harvard University Press.

Kovacs, David. 1994–2002. *Euripides*. Loeb Classical Library. Cambridge MA: Harvard University Press.

Lloyd-Jones, Hugh. 1994. *Sophocles*. Loeb Classical Library. Cambridge MA: Harvard University Press.

Mikalson, Jon D. 1975. *The Sacred and Civil Calendar of the Athenian Year*. Princeton: Princeton University Press.

Most, Glenn W. 2013. "The Madness of Tragedy." In *Mental Disorders in the Classical World*, edited by William V. Harris, 395–410. Leiden: Brill.

Pickard-Cambridge, Arthur. ²1968. *The Dramatic Festivals of Athens*, second edition rev. John Gould and D. M. Lewis. Oxford: Clarendon Press.

Rau, Peter. 1967. *Paratragodia: Untersuchung einer komischen Form des Aristophanes*. Munich: C. H. Beck.

Robortello, Francesco. 1968. *In librum Aristotelis de arte poetica explanationes* (Florentiae: In officina Laurentii Torrentini ducalis typographi, 1548); reprint: Munich: W. Fink.

Schwindt, Jürgen Paul. 1994. *Das Motiv der "Tagesspanne": Ein Beitrag zur Ästhetik der Zeitgestaltung im griechisch-römischen Drama*. Paderborn: F. Schöningh.

Anke Walter
Festive Time in the Poetry of Horace

Introduction

Among Roman authors, the poet Horace (65–8 BCE) offers profound insights into festive time.[1] According to his *Odes*, festive time can have essentially two different shapes: it can be perceived as a highly precious, but also a highly fleeting moment, or, as we see in the context of public festivity in particular, it can be a moment when the Romans – and their poet – are fully in possession of all time, of their past, present, and future. The way the individual in Horace's lyric poetry experiences festive time in the short span of their lives, then, is very different from the way the Roman citizen experiences public festive time, with Rome's long history that it evokes and the promise that Rome will last well into the future, with the blessing of its gods.

Both kinds of festive experience are juxtaposed within the *Odes*, but on one occasion they are also brought in immediate contact within one and the same poem. In *Odes* 3.8 and 2.11, we shall see how Horace sets up festivity as a highly precious, yet ultimately fleeting moment in time. Preparations are necessary in order to bring about the festive moment, when the wine and the decorations are in place, music is being played, and the guests are gathered and have let go of the worries of everyday and public life, ready to celebrate. This moment, which in Horace's poetry is not so much fully present but forever only just about to become a reality, is presented by Horace as an antidote against the swift passage of time and human life, including the short-lived joys of youth, beauty, and love. But, as we shall see, the precious festive moment can never be fully subtracted from the passage of time, which does leave its traces even on the festivities themselves.

In *Ode* 3.14, the private and the public experience of festivity interact in an intriguing way within the space of one and the same poem. In *Ode* 4.6, which takes up several of the themes of Horace's famous *carmen saeculare*, Horace presents

---

[1] For festivals in Horace, see e.g. *Odes* 1.21; 1.36; 2.11; 2.12.17–20; 3.8; 3.14; 3.17; 3.18; 3.23; 3.28; 4.6; 4.11; see Lieberg (1965); Feeney (1993, 58–60); Tringali (1995, 17–46); Griffin (1997); Evans (2023). For the pervasive character of festivity in Book 4, closely connected with the theme of time and its passage, see Putnam (1986, 314–317); Krasser (2008), with an emphasis on Horace's triumph poems. This does not mean, however, that Horace's festive poems would have to be tied to any actual religious or festive events; see Fraenkel (1957, 381; 404); Schmidt (1980, 31).

Open Access. © 2024 the author(s), published by De Gruyter. [CC BY-NC-ND] This work is licensed under the Creative Commons Attribution-NonCommercial-NoDerivatives 4.0 International License.
https://doi.org/10.1515/9783111366876-004

himself as the master of a festive ceremony that comprises and celebrates the fullness of Roman time, bringing together in his poem Rome's past, present, and future. He memorably invokes the gods to secure their protection, and by weaving together many different aspects of time – the linear and the cyclical, the time of history, of nature, of genealogical succession, of Roman "ages" (*saecula*) and poetic immortality – he invites his audience to partake in a profound kind of "thick", highly meaningful festive moment, on which Horace explicitly predicates his own immortal poetic fame. The "fullness" of time that scholars like Jan Assmann have singled out as a key feature of festive time (see introduction) can thus be seen at work in Horace's poetry. The festive time evoked here seems much more solid and stable, far removed from the precious, yet fleeting character of festive time that is reflected in the other festive and sympotic odes. Horace, then, is well aware of the double nature of festive time as well as of its aesthetic literary potential, as he immortalizes both of its aspects in his eternal poetry.

1 *Carmen* 3.8

Ode 3.8 is a good case study for Horace's construction of festivity as a precious moment, one that is only just about to fully become a reality, yet one that is still, by virtue of Horace's art, immortalized through poetry. The ode is firmly set on a festive day: the first of March, the festival of the Matronalia.[2] This day has a special meaning both for the women (*matronae*) of Rome, but also for Horace himself, since this was a crucial day of his life when he was almost killed by a falling tree, but survived: he says that, on this day, he was "almost sent to his grave by the blow of a tree" (3.8.7–8).[3] Different public and private meanings, then, converge on this day. The poem starts off with a vivid setting of the scene, couched in the form of a dialogue, when Horace says that his addressee – who is only in line 13 revealed to be Maecenas – might be wondering "what the flowers mean, and the casket full of incense, and the charcoal laid on the altar of fresh-cut turf" (2–4). Everything seems to be ready, so that the party can begin.

---

[2] On this ode, see Fraenkel (1957, 221–223); Syndikus (1973, 103–109); Schmidt (1980, 26–28); Lyne (1995, 109–111); Thom (2008, 51). – For the festival of the Matronalia referred to here, see Nisbet and Rudd (2004, ad loc.).

[3] Text: Shackleton Bailey (1995); translations: Rudd (2004). – For this incident, see also *carm.* 2.13; 2.17.27–32; 3.4.27; Oppermann (1980, 172–178). For intriguing comments on how Horace in this and other odes intertwines public and private festive occasions, mimicking Augustus' own approach to festivals, to guarantee his own memory, see Evans (2023). On anticipation in *carmen* 3.8, see Barber (2014, 351–352).

The same applies to the wine, which is almost an icon of Horace's festive and sympotic poetry, one that can make the celebrants forget their cares and enjoy the moment, but that can also, depending on its age and the year when it was produced, convey historical memories.⁴ In this case, the wine, which comes from a jar "that was first taught to drink the smoke in Tullus' consulship" (11–12),⁵ will mark the beginning of the festivities, when the festal day itself, "as the year comes round, will remove the cork, with its seal of pitch, from the jar" (9–11).⁶ The poet then tells Maecenas to "quaff a hundred ladles, in honour of your friend's escape, and keep the lamps burning until daylight" (13–15). Once more, then, Horace underlines the notion that everything is prepared and that the celebration could begin right now.

Throughout the poem, Horace keeps talking to his addressee. This too underscores the festive atmosphere and suggests that both the host and his guest are being present, so that the festivities can start right away. Yet this never happens. While it is possible to form a detailed mental image of what the festivities are going to look like, these never become a reality described in the present indicative, but they are exclusively expressed through imperatives addressed to Maecenas or predictions in the future tense.⁷ Throughout, then, the full realisation of the festive moment with its drinking and the carelessness and joy that comes with it is deferred: it is forever imminent, without, it seems, ever reaching the moment of its actual fulfilment.⁸

---

4 The meaning of the different wines in Horace's *Odes* has been much discussed; see Commager (1957); Schmidt (1980); Bradshaw (2002, 6–7); Davis (2007).
5 The seeming exactitude of this phrase also belies the fact that it is not at all clear whether Horace is here referring to L. Volcacius Tullus, consul of 33 BC, or his father of the same name, consul of 66 BC; Schmidt (1980, 26–28); Lyne (1995, 110 n. 40), and Nisbet and Rudd (2004, ad loc.) convincingly opt for the former; Nisbet and Hubbard (1978, 201–202), however, leave the matter open.
6 Schmidt (1980, 27) makes a good case for not taking this phrase to mean that this was the first anniversary of the incident, but that it happened in 33 BC and was thus coeval with the wine served on the occasion of this anniversary; see also Nisbet and Hubbard (1970, who date 3.8 to 25 BC: p. xxix; xxxiii; 244).
7 For the pervasive role of the imperative in Horace's sympotic poems as well as the use of the future tense, see Barber (2014, esp. 339–355); for Horace's use of the future tense in sympotic poems with "the illocutionary force of exhortation", see Davis (1991, 160–163); also Syndikus (1972, 214); Lyne (1995, 108 n. 28); *contra* Fraenkel (1957, 214; 221–222 on 1.20).
8 In a slightly different way, Lowrie (1997, 54) too speaks of "a moment of anticipation rather than fulfilment" evoked by the sympotic-erotic imagery of *Ode* 1.4; see also the excellent analysis of this ode by Corbeill (1994). Cf. Barber (2014), who argues that Horace, particularly in the sympotic poems, deploys directives and verbs in the future tense "to problematize rather than affirm presence and to dramatize rather than compass the fleeting and continuous nature of time" (p. 334); Lieberg (1965, 411); for the role of the future tense in Horace's amatory odes, see Rumpf (2017). –

What Horace does describe in *carmen* 3.8 as a present reality, in contrast to the fulfilment of the festive moment that is merely anticipated, is the current situation of Rome and the empire. After telling Maecenas to keep the lamp burning until daylight, the poet wishes that all "shouting and quarrelling" should be far away. Maecenas himself should cast aside his worries for the capital and its citizens (15–17). The lines that follow (17–24) are set apart not only by their subject matter – the "shouting and quarrelling" of Rome's public life and Rome's wars with her external enemies – but also by the time frame that they inhabit. While the fulfilment of the festive moment itself is deferred, although the day in question is definitely "there" (cf. *hic dies*, 9), the political situation in the Roman empire, of which Maecenas is asked to banish all thoughts, is described as a present reality, with present indicative verbs: the Medes are torn apart by internal warfare, the Cantabrians are Rome's slaves, the Scythians prepare to withdraw from the plains (*dissidet*; *servit*; *meditantur*, 20–23). The present state of affairs in Rome and the empire, then, is set off against the intense focus on the imminent festive moment itself.

At the same time, both spheres are closely interwoven: with the poet's choice to spend two stanzas on the details of the situation throughout the empire, rather than admonishing Maecenas in very general terms not to worry about it, this wider context is activated as a foil for the festive moment. And yet, the close connection of these two spheres creates a tension on which the poem rests and which is nicely captured in the final two lines: *dona praesentis cape laetus horae, / linque severa* ("gladly accept the gifts of the present hour, and let serious things go hang", 27–28).[9] The poem's last word, *severa*, harks back to the worries of the political state of affairs, both internally and externally – even though Maecenas is asked to leave these behind (*linque*), their very presence is reasserted with the poem's last word.

The injunction in the preceding line explicitly draws attention to the "present hour", or the present festive moment around which the poem revolves. However, as long as Maecenas' worries about Roman politics are still present as well – and as long as the thought of them is reinforced by the poem's last word – that festive

---

Horace's *Odes* here certainly tie in with his Greek lyric predecessors: in Greek lyric poetry too it is almost a commonplace to depict imminent moments of festivity in the future tense or using imperatives or cohortatives – to say "let us drink" rather than "here we are, drinking" (cf. e.g. Alc. fr. 346). For representations of the Greek banquet in art, but also in poetry, see Lissarrague (1987). See also Nisbet and Hubbard (1978, on carm. 2.11, p. 168–169); Nisbet and Hubbard (1970, 402; 421–422).

9 For the crucial role played by the *carpe diem* motif in Horace's poetry, see Syndikus (1972, 74–75 with 75 n. 25); Davis (1991, 145–188); for its role in Horace's festive poems, see Lieberg (1965); for the image of the rose in the context of the *carpe diem* motif, see Lee (1969, 55; 90–102); Gold (1993).

moment will remain what it is throughout *Ode* 3.8: an anticipation forever deferred rather than actually fulfilled within the framework of this poem. By reinforcing, at the end, both what this poem sketches out in detail and leads us to expect as well as the "serious things" that stand in the way of festive fulfilment, this very oscillation between expectation and deferral is fixed as one of the essential principles on which this festive poem rests. The idea of deferred festive fulfilment, then, not only resides in the imperative forms and future tenses of this poem, but is firmly written into its very structure. Horace thus creates a moment full of tension and anticipation, a moment that communicates with, but that is truly lifted above ordinary, historical time. The fact that this day is being celebrated by Horace because it is, in a sense, his second birthday, gives the poem a metapoetic dimension, reminding us of the power of the poet and his poetry, which outlasts the poet himself and immortalizes even the vivid sense of festive anticipation that this poem projects.

2 *Carmen* 2.11

For Horace, festive time and the questions that it raises are by no means restricted to individual days on the calendar, but it represents a more general feature of human existence. Festive elements recur again and again throughout the *Odes*, in the sympotic poems:[10] these could be just drinking and community, or they could involve more elaborate elements like flowers, the use of costly oil, and the presence of beautiful girls.[11] In contrast to poems set on a specific date, such as 3.8, the sympotic poems, of which I shall discuss *carmen* 2.11 as a representative example, focus on a day that is not "on record", i.e., a day that is not meant for commemoration, either public or private, and that has no clear identity and place in the calendar.

In *Ode* 2.11, just as in 3.8, Horace sets the spirit of festivity off against the present political situation.[12] He starts by telling his addressee Quinctius to "leave off

---

[10] For Horace's so-called "meta-sympotic" poems, see Mindt (2007); for the "poetics of presence" in Horace's *Odes*, see Lowrie (1997, 19–76); Mindt (2007, esp. 80–84); Gramps (2021, esp. 99–104); for Horace's ethics of *nunc*, see Syndikus (1972, 74–75); for the temporality of Horace's amatory odes, see Ancona (1994).

[11] For the characteristic features and ethical implications of Horace's sympotic poems, see Davis (1991); Davis (2007).

[12] On 2.11, see Syndikus (1972, 404–409); Lowrie (1997, 87); Sutherland (2002, 118–125); for its connection with 2.9, see Santirocco (1986, 91–93). On anticipation in *carmen* 2.11, see Barber (2014, 351).
– For the pervasive presence of Anacreontic themes in the ode, see Harrison (2017, 135–136).

asking what the warmongering Cantabrian is plotting and the Scythian, who is separated from us by the barrier of the Adriatic" (2.11.1–3). The poet reminds Quinctius that he should not "fuss about the needs of our short life, for there is little that it requires" (3–5), and that youth and beauty disappear quickly, as well as "wild love affairs and easy sleep" (5–8). Similarly, the beauty of spring flowers fades, and the moon does not "always shine with the same glowing face" (9–11).[13] He concludes this first half of the poem by saying that there is no point in "wearing out your brain (which isn't up to it) with plans that stretch to infinity" (11–12). Given the fleeting nature of time, Horace asks why they do not sit down "beneath a tall plane tree, or better this pine here, while there is still time", smear their hair with Syrian nard and garland themselves with "sweet-scented roses" (13–17). This question, together with the deictic reference to "this pine tree here" (*sub* [...] *hac* / *pinu*, 13–14) and the reminder of the passage of time (*dum licet*, 16),[14] suggests that this is or at least could be happening in the present moment.

Other elements of festivity, by contrast, are again deferred: after stating that "Euhius dispels gnawing anxieties" (17–18), the poet asks which of the slave-boys will be the first to mix the cups of Falernian wine with fresh water and who will entice the prostitute Lyde from her house (18–22). As in 3.8, Horace then again uses imperatives to depict what should happen: the slave should tell her "to grab her ivory lyre and hurry up, tying her uncombed hair in a knot, Spartan style" (22–24). The fulfilment of the festive moment, then, is again only anticipated and not yet fully present.[15] However, throughout the ode Horace gives many detailed graphic hints at what the festive moment is going to look and feel like once it is finally there, so that this moment can take on a life of its own in the hearts and minds of Horace's audience, whom the poem invites again and again to enjoy the sweet sense of festive anticipation, in the face of the quick and merciless passage of the time of human life.

Yet what is also striking about this festive moment is the hurry with which the preparations need to be completed: the poet asks which of the slave-boys will dilute the wine with fresh water "faster" (*quis puer ocius*, 18), and he tells one of

---

13 For the moon as "a frequent Horatian symbol of change and a celestial body linked by the ancients with fertility and rejuvenation", see Corbeill (1994, 98–99 with n. 14).
14 For the idea in Horace that one needs to enjoy life while one can, see Harrison (2017, ad loc.); Nisbet and Hubbard (1970, ad 1.9.16, 17).
15 Sutherland (2002, 124) too notes the sense of suspension at the end of *Ode* 2.11: "[T]he poet creates Lyde as "desirable female" for his audience, then leaves her in suspension, ever out of our reach. This suspension of her arrival means that the party of 2.11 never quite ends. We remain in a potentially permanent state of *carpe diem*, always waiting for Lyde to finish putting up her hair and appear at the gathering."

them to go and tell the prostitute to hurry up (*dic, age,* [...] *maturet,* 22–23).[16] The aside that one needs to celebrate "while it is still time" (*dum licet,* 16) is thus fully brought to life: since time flies by so fast, there does not seem to be much time to waste in getting the celebrations under way. While the two halves of *Ode* 2.11 neatly juxtapose the themes of the swift passage of time and the sympotic enjoyment of the moment, which seems just about to fully begin, it turns out that the supposed contrast between the two is not quite so neat after all. When Horace says that he and his addressee should garland their grey hair with sweet-scented roses (*rosa / canos odorati capillos,* 14–15), it is hard not to hear an echo of his previous statement that dry grey hair drives off wild love affairs (*arida / pellente lascivos amores / canitie,* 6–8) and that "the beauty of spring flowers does not last forever" (9–10). With this in mind, the focus on the prostitute at the end of the poem itself becomes a reminder that the enjoyment of such a "wild love affair" is fleeting, particularly since the poet and his addressee are – humorously – described as grey-haired (15).[17] Finally, it is probably no coincidence that in a poem on the fleeting nature of time the fresh water of a stream is referred to as *praeteriens lympha* (20). The very drink that Horace and Quinctius will enjoy, the "burning Falernian" (*ardentis Falerni,* 19) mixed with that water, embodies what *Ode* 2.11 is all about: that time, like the fresh water from the stream, keeps flowing by.

The girl's hair style too, the final image of the poem, is fitting for this context: she is to "hurry up, tying her uncombed hair in a knot, Spartan style" (22–24). Apparently, then, there is no time to comb the hair and to arrange it in any more complex way than a simple Spartan "bun".[18] The festive moment, then, is characterized by the haste with which it has to start, dictated by the fleeting nature of time and the fast approach of death, as well as by the very beauty of that moment that is soon to come. As the vivid image of Lyde in her simple Spartan hairstyle suggests, the specific kind of this festive beauty and the dictates of time under which it stands are inextricably intertwined. While the poet suggests celebration as the one antidote against time's swift passage, what he creates is not a "timeless" moment that would give us respite from the pressing nature of time, but a moment

---

16 For the importance and meaning of the "'hurry up' motif" in Horace's sympotic odes, see Davis (2016, 278–281).
17 For the amusing reversal of *pellente lascivos amores / canitie* (7–8) in the invitation to Lyde in the concluding stanza, see Harrison (2017, ad 6–8); for the humour, see also Nisbet and Hubbard (1978, ad 15). – For correspondences and contrasts between the two halves of the ode, see Syndikus (1972, 408); Nisbet and Hubbard (1978, 168); Harrison (2017, 135).
18 For this type of coiffure and its association with haste and simplicity, see Nisbet and Hubbard (1978, ad loc.), who also comment (p. 169–179) on the characteristic interplay, throughout this ode, of luxury and simplicity, the cheap and the exquisite; Harrison (2017, ad loc.).

that is beautiful precisely because it very openly has to be snatched from the hands of time.

Here, we can also see why it is so important that Horace depicts the festive moment the way he does, through creating a vivid sense of anticipation rather than narrating what is a present reality: were the festive moment actually present, it would just as quickly fade into the past, given that time, as the imagery of *carmen* 2.11 suggests, keeps on passing even during a festival. By casting this moment as eternally in the future and thus as one that has not yet fully begun, however, Horace, as it were, rescues it from time. In the face of the swift passage of time, which also leaves its mark on the festive preparations that need to happen quickly, Horace again and again invites us to vividly imagine a festive moment that is just about to begin, with his poetic artistry that will forever keep this moment alive for us, through a vivid sense of anticipation. As such, Horace indeed makes this intensely focused, suspended moment truly immortal: as he himself emphasizes e.g. in 3.30, his poetry is eternal[19] – its art consisting in the fact that it can bring back eternally the same sense of how swiftly time passes, both the time of life and the time of the festival. The festive moment that Horace constructs, then, is of a very special nature: it is both vivid and insubstantial, and the poetic form guarantees its eternity, while it is actually not more than the sweet anticipation of a fleeting moment as part of a life that is just as fleeting. Interestingly for our purposes, this moment, for Horace, is also not firmly tied to the calendar, but it can come about in any sympotic setting, at any time – it is not so much the calendar itself that creates such festive moments, but the human need to enjoy life while one still can, in the face of the all-too-swift passage of time.

3 *Carmen* 3.14

In both 3.8 and 2.11, we saw how the outside world of Roman military affairs and politics is figured as inimical to the fulfilment of the festive moment and the beginning of true festive joy. As we shall now see, however, this is only true for the day-to-day business of the state: public life too can have its festive days, which, in *Ode* 3.14, even interact directly with festivity in the private sphere. The ode is dedicated to the public celebration of Augustus' return from a victorious campaign in Spain, in the spring or early summer of 24 BC, and in its second

---

19 For the eternity of Horace's poetry, see Feeney (1993, esp. 50–54); Barchiesi (1996); Lowrie (1997, esp. 70–76); Feeney (2016) for "Horace's new obsession in Book 4 with the power of his poetry to confer immortality" (p. 312).

half describes the poet's own, personal celebration on the same occasion.[20] Again, the deferral of the festive moment has an important role to play in this context. While focusing attention on the seemingly imminent moment when the festivity is fully going to begin, the poet at the same time manages to open up that intensely focused time for a range of recollections, both public and private. The two spheres are closely intertwined, while it also becomes clear that they reflect two rather different ways of experiencing festivity itself: as a fleeting and precious moment, or as a monumental embodiment of security and stability that is going to last well into the future.

The poem starts by naming the festive occasion that gives rise to this ode in the first place: Augustus' return from Spain. As though he were directing a festive ceremony, Horace[21] then gives orders for what should happen next, in the subjunctive: Augustus' wife Livia should come forth, "performing due ritual to the righteous gods" (3.14.6), his sister, as well as, just as "adorned with suppliant garlands", the mothers of young men and women who were recently saved from death (7–10). Finally, the poet addresses boys and girls "who have had no experience of a man" and tells them to "avoid any words of ill omen" (11–12). With this, the stage for the public celebration is set, and it looks as though, with the festive community assembled and the command to avoid words of ill omen being given,[22] the ceremony could now move on to the culminating event, such as the advent of Augustus himself.[23]

---

[20] On *Ode* 3.14, see Fraenkel (1957, 288–291); Syndikus (1973, 142–153); Schmidt (1980, 20–22); Lyne (1995, 169–173); Morgan (2005); on anticipation in *carmen* 3.14, see Barber (2014, 354–355); Carey (2016, 187–189); for the connection of 3.14 with 3.8, see Santirocco (1986, 128–131). – On the interplay of public and private layers of meaning in Horace's poetry, see also Syndikus (1972, 404–405); Santirocco (1986, 110–131); Corbeill (1994, esp. 103–106) on 1.44; Lowrie (1997, esp. 345–349) for the conclusion of this interplay in carm. 4.15.

[21] Strictly speaking, however, the identity of the speaker in the first three stanzas is not clear; as Fraenkel (1957, 290–291) rightly points out, it is a "nondescript figure" and could be either "a kind of herald" or "some such anonymous character". Yet since, from the fourth stanza onwards, it becomes very clear that the speaking voice is the poet's and since throughout the poem the speaker essentially fulfils the same function – giving commands for the festive procedures – I take it that the poet, even though his identity is unveiled only in the middle of the poem, is the speaker throughout.

[22] For a similar function of the command to hold holy silence at the beginning of a ceremony, see e.g. also Call. Hymn. Ap. 17 (εὐφημεῖτ' ἀίοντες ἐπ' Ἀπόλλωνος ἀοιδῇ) or Tib. 2.2.1–2; Ov. Trist. 5.5.5–6; further parallels are collected by Syndikus (1973, 148 n. 31).

[23] For the nature of this ceremony, with features both of an *adventus* and a *supplicatio*, see Nisbet and Rudd (2004, 180–181). Syndikus (1973, 143 with n. 12) reads it as a "Dankopfer" on the occasion of Augustus' return, offered by the women of the imperial household and the Roman matrons; see also Fraenkel (1957, 289); Lyne (1995, 170) classifies it as *descriptio triumphi*.

At this point, however, the poet states that this day, which for him is truly festal, will dispel his "black worries" (13–14), since he will not be afraid "of insurrection or violent death while Caesar is in charge of the world" (14–16). With this move away from the scene of the sacred ceremony, the poet, in the middle stanza of the poem, ushers in the turn to what looks like the poet's private celebration of this day that takes up the second half of the ode.[24] The transition from one sphere to the next is marked by the motif of the wine, which Horace wants to drink at his private symposium, but which has an eminently political and historical meaning as well. As in 2.11, the poet addresses a slave-boy (*puer*), telling him to go and look for scented ointment, garlands, "and a jar that remembers the Marsian War" (17–20). What is new here, however, is the fact that now, a condition is introduced, for the poet continues, "if there is anywhere a crock that has managed to elude the marauding Spartacus" (18–20).[25] The festive moment, then, is not only deferred, but tied to a condition – even one that it seems fairly hard to meet.

Secondly, the boy is to "tell the clear-voiced Neaera to hurry up, tying a band around her myrrh-scented hair. If any delay occurs on account of the odious doorman, come away" (21–24). Again, as in 2.11, we are reminded of the speed with which the preparations for the festive moment need to happen (cf. *properet*). These preparations are urgent and cannot tolerate any delay (cf. *mora*). With Neaera's characterisation as "clear-voiced" (*argutae*) and the reference to her "myrrh-scented hair", the poet gives his audience a glimpse of the sensory pleasures to be expected from her participation in the celebration, but – not unlike the wine to be brought to the celebrations – it is also made clear how rare and fleeting these pleasures are and how much they depend on the correct timing: in this case, this is not the wine's origin during a particular couple of years and its having survived a destructive event in between, but rather the swiftness with which the young girl needs to come and her ability to avoid any delay. The emphasis is on speed rather than on old age and survival, but the main point – the crucial importance of the right timing – is the same.

The last stanza introduces a final temporal condition, referring to the poet's own lifetime. His grey hair, he states, "is mellowing my temper, which used to be eager for wrangling and impulsive brawls. I would not have put up with this sort of thing in my hot-blooded youth when Plancus was consul" (25–28). The festive moment that the poet has in mind, then, turns out to be possible only at a spe-

---

24 For the mediating function of this central stanza, see Fraenkel (1957, 290); Syndikus (1973, 149); for the turn at the centre of many of Horace's *Odes*, see Harrison (2004, esp. 88–90), for the "sympotic" turn in the middle of 3.14 and similar odes.
25 On the significance of the Social War, Spartacus, and the battle of Philippi, alluded to at the very end of the ode (see below), see Schmidt (1980, 21).

cific time in his life: his old age – when the tranquillity of that age only makes possible celebrations of this kind, presumably without picking a fight with the doorman who might delay Neaera's arrival.[26] Here again, as with the wine, a specific historical era is mentioned, anchoring the festive moment in a specific past: the year 42 BC, which, as Horace's readers would well know, was the year of the battle of Philippi.[27] These three stanzas together, then, underscore the need for the right timing, the many conditions that need to be met, and, thus, the rarity and precious nature of the festive moment that they anticipate.

The ode contains two different kinds of celebration – one public, one private – which are closely intertwined, but also contrasted at the same time. In the first half, the description of the festive ritual is of a strikingly monumental quality: the emperor's wife and sister are to step forth, as are the mothers of the young people recently saved from death; boys and unmarried young girls are to avoid words of ill omen. The persons involved here gain their significance from their relationship with the emperor as well as the recent past of their children, or the fact that they are still unmarried. A graphic detail that is provided is the fact that the mothers are "adorned with suppliant garlands" (*decorae / supplice vitta*, 7–8), otherwise the audience needs to imagine the relevant groups of people, of whose appearance no further details are known. The image that Horace evokes here parallels representations in art of sacrificial processions of the imperial family and other groups of people, such as on the – albeit much later – reliefs of the Ara Pacis,[28] as the scene exudes an air of sacredness and stability.

Horace's private festivity, by contrast, is much more dynamic, as is underlined by the imperatives, the need to speed up the preparations, and the emphasis on the exactly right timing and avoidance of delays. This sense of urgency is absent from the first half of the poem, with its more "stately" and monumental quality. The monumentality of the festive moment in the public sphere makes this an enduring and iconic scene, and the profound importance, not the uniqueness of this moment is stressed. By contrast, the poet's personal celebration foregrounds precisely this uniqueness, making the festive moment, if it will indeed come about the way the poet envisages it, a very rare occasion indeed, a highly precious moment in the stream of time that keeps inexorably moving on.

In a sense, the monumental stability of the festivities and the anticipation of one very specific and fleeting moment point to two rather different ways of experiencing the same festive occasion, even though the two are closely intertwined

---

26 For the theme of the poet's old age, see Fraenkel (1957, 414–416).
27 See Nisbet and Rudd (2004, ad loc.). – For the role played in this ode by these wars, evoked through the wine, see Fraenkel (1957, 290); Syndikus (1973, 152).
28 See also Syndikus (1973, 146–147) for this comparison.

and even though Horace's private celebration is predicated upon the turbulent history of the past and the new sense of stability. The same festive event can convey monumental stability or urgency, durability or a sense of the all-too-swift passage of time, which makes humans struggle to create the one perfect moment of festive *kairos*. In this ode, the two are not only connected through the fact that they take place on the same day, but both depend on each other to bring out the full meaning of this special day. On a small scale, the double character of the festivity depicted in this ode anticipates what we can observe in Horace's *Odes* at large, as we shall now see in the context of *carmen* 4.6. The festive moment, as *Ode* 3.14 shows us, is nothing absolute, but it is a specific experience of festive time that can look rather different, depending on whether it is located in the public or in the private sphere.

4 Horace as Master of Festive Time: *Ode* 4.6

The same poet who, in his odes on private festivity, makes it so memorably clear that it is impossible to grasp and hold on to the moment in its full festive completion, turns out to be a master of festive time in *Ode* 4.6 and the *Carmen saeculare*. Speaking as Roman *vates* and addressing the gods, in particular Apollo and Diana, he creates a festive moment and fills it with what seems like "all time": the time of history and nature, the time of linear progress and of ever-recurring cycles, of past, present, and future.[29] As a closer examination of *Ode* 4.6 will show, all these are made part of the festive moment in a poem that has its own tightly controlled rhythm and temporal structure and that adorns the festive moment with an air of monumentality and eternity.

Ode 4.6 is very clear in its structure and order of time.[30] It begins with an invocation of the god – Apollo, as it soon turns out – who took revenge on Niobe by killing her offspring as well as on Tityus who had tried to rape the god's mother Latona. The third of Apollo's victims listed here, Achilles, becomes the focus of the next four stanzas, which praise the hero's military prowess, while pointing

---

[29] On the role of cyclical recurrence in Horace's poetry, see Davis (1991) for the interplay of the circularity of natural and the linearity of human time; Corbeill (1994) on 1.4; also Rudd (1960).
[30] On carm. 4.6, see Fraenkel (1957, 400–407); Cairns (1971, 440–444); Syndikus (1973, 346–355); Putnam (1986, 115–130); Barchiesi (1996, 8–11); Lowrie (1997, 337–338); Hardie (1998); Miller (2009, 181–184; 288–297); Foster (2017); Phillips (2019); see Lowrie (2010, 213) for the structural importance of 4.6 within the fourth book of *Odes*, as marking the point where Horace's "arc of staged resistance" comes to an end; for Pindaric influence on *carmen* 4.6, see Fraenkel (1957, 400–403); Barchiesi (1996, 8–11); Hardie (1998); Foster (2017); for Horace's relationship with Vergil in 4.6, see Feeney (2016, 305–307).

to the darker sides of his character, such as a tendency to excessive cruelty. This hero, in Horace's version of the myth, had to be reigned in by Apollo, since Jupiter had followed Venus' wishes and decided that Aeneas should escape from the destruction of Troy to found new city walls (21–24). With this central stanza, the poem turns to Apollo, who is addressed again in lines 25–28. Mirroring the transition from Troy to Rome with the figure of Aeneas, Apollo too seems to make that transition: the poet first states that the god "washes his hair in Xanthus' stream", i.e. in Troy, and in the next line he is asked to "protect the glory of the Daunian (i.e., Roman) Muse" (26–27).[31] This move also prepares us for the transition from Homeric material to a reference to the poet himself, since Apollo is then declared to be the source of the poet's song: the one who "gave me inspiration, who gave me the lyric art and the name of poet" (29–30). After the world of myth and of Rome's prehistory, then, the poet turns to his own "prehistory", i.e., the origin and source of his becoming a poet in the first place.

In the next lines, Horace, as though following the chain of poetic creation that begins with the god of song and continues with himself as inspired poet, addresses the members of the chorus who perform his ode, as "you, the foremost of our maidens, and you, the sons of noble sires" (31–32). Again, there is an emphasis on origin, in this case the noble origin of the youths (*puerique claris / patribus orti*), which underscores the way the poem and the moment of its performance are anchored in the past: in the history of Troy and Rome's foundation, in the poet's initiation into the poetic art by his patron Apollo, as well as in the noble birth of the young people forming the choir. Horace orders the members of the choir to "observe the Lesbian beat and the snap of my fingers" as they sing of Apollo and Diana (35–36).[32] With the "Lesbian beat" (*Lesbium pedem*), the poet invokes another line of tradition: the poetic tradition of Sappho's verse and the metre that he uses so frequently, imitating it in his own Latin *Odes*. Together, all of these traditions stand behind the metrical "time" of this poem, i.e., its distinctive rhythm of long and short syllables and the rhythm of its stanzas: Apollo, Sappho, the poet Horace, as well as the chorus whose task it is to bring that beat to life and to set the poet's words to the snapping of his fingers. The very rhythm of the poem, then, is both a sign of the past – a product of previous poets with the bless-

---

[31] For the "bending" of the ode at this point ("from Achilles dead to Aeneas surviving, from the ill-omened walls of Troy to the auspicious ramparts of Rome, from the mythic past to the lived present" and of Apollo from Far-darter to Lyre-Player and Leader of the Muses, p. 120), see Putnam (1986, 120–121); Foster (2017, 159–160); for this important transitional moment in the poem, see also Miller (2009, 292–293).

[32] For the meaning of these lines, see the discussions in Fraenkel (1957, 403–404); Thomas (2011, ad loc.).

ing of the god of poetry himself – and an emblem of the present moment, marking the very rhythm that structures time while this ode is being recited.

When Horace tells the choir to duly praise Diana in song, the focus shifts from images of linear to those of cyclical time, as Diana is called "the Nightlighter with her crescent torch, who gives increase to our crops and swiftly rolls the hurrying months" (38–40).[33] In the last stanza of the poem, it becomes clear that the young women of the choir too are part of this cycle of life and nature. The poet addresses one of them, saying "in due course, as a married lady, you will say 'when the cycle brought round its festal days, I performed the hymn to please the gods, having learned the tune from its eminent composer: Horace'" (*nupta iam dices "ego dis amicum, / saeculo festas referente luces, / reddidi carmen, docilis modorum / vatis Horati*, 41–44). The "foremost of the maidens" (*virginum primae*, 31) of the choir, then, will become married women (*nuptae*) and in their turn give birth to a new generation.[34] By placing his own name at the very end of the ode, in an imagined speech by the female members of the choir, spoken at a time in the future when the *virgines* will have become *nuptae*, Horace includes his poem right in the middle of this cycle of time: of growing older, moving from one stage of life to the next, including the prospect of the coming of the next generation.

The fact that the married women will say that they performed a Horatian *carmen* "when the cycle brought rounds its festal days" (*saeculo festas referente luces*) closely connects this ode with the *Carmen saeculare* (quite literally and self-consciously "bringing back" the memory of that poem, cf. *referente*)[35] performed four years before the publication of Horace's fourth book of *Odes*.[36] The young men and women who are about to end their performance of *Ode* 4.6, we learn here, were the same who performed the secular hymn in honour of the same gods, Apollo and Diana. The last stanza of this poem, then, becomes a unique kind of double sphragis ("seal"), sealing both the *Carmen saeculare* and *Ode* 4.6 with a reference to the chorus and the name of the poet. This imitates and repeats the reference to "the chorus trained to sing in praise of Phoebus and Diana" at the

---

[33] For the role of Diana at the end of this ode, see Miller (2009, 295).
[34] For the connection between Apollo, the *vates* Horace, and the members of the choir, as well as for the importance of the theme of teaching in this poem, see Putnam (1986, 121; 123; 129). On the sphragis, see Feeney (1998, 37 n. 82); Thomas (2011, ad 4.6.44).
[35] For another, similarly self-conscious echo, see Thomas (2011, ad 4.6.41–44), "appropriately the girl 'echoes' the text of the CS"; see also Miller (2009, 296–297).
[36] For the relationship of *Ode* 4.6 with the *Carmen saeculare*, see Barchiesi (1996, 8–9); Putnam (2000, 99–103); Putnam (2010, 245–246); Phillips (2019, 438–444); Thomas (2011, on 31–32; 41–44; 41–43; 42; 43) for the verbal parallels between 4.6 and the *Carmen saeculare*; Phillips (2019, 439 n. 46).

end of the secular song itself (*doctus et Phoebi chorus et Dianae / dicere laudes*, carm. saec. 75–76; cf. *docilis modorum*, carm. 4.6.43) and completes it by naming the poet who is not mentioned by name in the *Carmen saeculare*, in fact, not anywhere else in his collection of *Odes*.[37] *Ode* 4.6, then, becomes a kind of "postlude" to the saecular song, making that poem's ideas of time and of poetry fully at home in the *Odes* themselves. This self-conscious reference also underlines the poetic rhythm that is created as Horace takes his audience back to the same festive spirit and the same metre as the poem that was performed in the context of the Secular Games a few years previously. Like the cycles of nature and human life, this festive moment itself becomes a repeated phenomenon, enacting and praising once more the well-ordered character of Rome's present time.

At the end of this ode it is again striking that we have another future tense, this time marking not what Horace himself, but what the married woman will say: *dices* (41). This future, however, is rather different from the future of the festive poems examined earlier. Since we are here dealing with the naming of a name, the statement quoted here, although it is to be spoken in the future, is already doing its work in the present, since it reminds us of the poet's name, ties it to the work, and preserves its fame for the future. Instead of deferring a festive moment to the future, then, this future tense here spans several layers of time: it seals the *Carmen saeculare* and *Ode* 4.6, marking the completion of this group of poems, it impresses us in the present moment with the poet's name, and it guarantees the future of that very name, by stating that it will indeed be pronounced in the future. The future tense of *dices*, then, actually shows that Horace's fame is indeed already living through time.

The poet whom we encounter here is in full mastery of time – of the metre and the rhythm of his poem, of his literary tradition, both epic and lyric, of Rome's history, and the natural order of time. He does not shy away from starting the poem with an invocation of Apollo (*dive*) and sealing it with his own name (*vatis Horati*), emphasizing his own position in the ordered world of time and poetry guaranteed by this god, who first gave him the name of poet (*Phoebus artem / carminis nomenque dedit poetae*, 29–30).[38] This ring structure underscores the notion of closure, but also of the monumentality and immortality of this poem. In *Ode* 4.6, Horace creates a festive atmosphere and celebrates the festive moment in which he and the chorus honour these gods, evoking many different layers of time and their ordered working. The poet brings past, present, and future to

---

37 Cf. Putnam (1986, 122–123 with 123 n. 14) for the passages in Horace's other works where he does refer to his *nomen* or *cognomen*.
38 See Miller (2009, 297) for this sphragis and how Horace here "artfully inscribes the message of his own and the 'Apolline' *Carmen*'s achievement in another *carmen* to Apollo."

bear on this festive moment, making it a very rich moment and one infused with profound meaning, as the poem invites reflection on and celebrates Rome's past, present, and future, as well as the divine blessing it has been enjoying and – with the poet's help – will keep enjoying as generation follows upon generation. There is a clear contrast, then, between the poems dedicated to private festivity, as examined earlier, and *Ode* 4.6, as Horace either creates eternal snapshots of the deferral of the full festive moment in its fleeting character or composes a festive poem that infuses the festive moment with, it seems, all of time, anchoring it in several layers and kinds of time and creating a particularly dense moment, one that seems much more solid, recurring with almost natural necessity, than the precious and fleeting moments of private festivity.

Conclusion

Overall, then, we have seen two kinds of festivity in the *Odes* and *Carmen saeculare*. The poet's own private celebrations remain strikingly deferred to the future, through imperatives and future tenses. In *carmen* 3.8, the contrast between this moment of the immediate future and that which is described in the present tense – the situation throughout Rome's *imperium* – is particularly striking. This kind of festivity, for Horace, is not limited to the actual festive days marked on a private or public calendar, but it can occur at any point, as depicted in the sympotic odes, such as *Ode* 2.11. In *carmen* 3.14, the expectation of the private festive moment comes in direct contact with the much less dynamic, monumental moment of public festivity. The contrast between the two spheres that is so characteristic for Horace's lyric oeuvre at large is thus anchored within Books 1–3 of the *Odes* themselves. In *Ode* 4.6, as well as the *Carmen saeculare*, finally, Horace styles himself as the poet of the full, lived, and present festive moment, which he fills with profound meaning and many different images and layers of time. He uses this also to foreground his own name in *Carmen* 4.6, self-consciously writing it both into the present and the future, making it part of the cyclical recurrence of the generations.

Both kinds of festive time are equally made eternal in Horace's poetry. The main difference between them is the perspective from which they view time. Seen from the point of view of the Roman state with its long history and the protection of the gods that it has been enjoying, according to Horace, the poet and his contemporaries can be relatively certain of time: if the gods remain propitious, the cycle of time will continue, there will be further Secular Games, and generation will keep following on generation, like a law of nature. For the *individuum*, by contrast, the present moment can be the last, the present festive day can, but need not, be followed by another – even if, as we saw in *carmen* 3.14, the safety of the empire is now guaranteed by Augustus' successful return.

In the connection of these two different approaches can lie both a warning and a salutary message. On the one hand, if one reads the *Carmen saeculare* and *Ode* 4.6 with Horace's previous festive poems in mind, one is reminded that even what the *vates* fashions as such a powerful moment of ordered festive time, apparently grounded in all of time and the will of the gods, is for the individuum still only the most fleeting moment of a life that will soon be lived, only one of the many short-lived human joys. On the other hand, a Roman could find comfort in this juxtaposition of two kinds of festivity: even though the individual life is so short, Rome itself has lived and will go on living for much longer, the cycles of Roman time will continue. The individual life becomes just one more bridge between Rome's glorious past and future. Horace addresses his audience both as fellow human beings and as Roman citizens and makes it clear that these two identities entail two different ways of experiencing festive time. The contrast between the two cannot fully be resolved and is itself part of human existence and of festivity, which can bring out both the most enduring and the most ephemeral aspects of that existence. The *vates* Horace predicates his own poetic immortality at least in part on his ability to convey in equally haunting ways both the ephemerality of the individual and the eternity of the community, of which festivals can remind us all.

References

Ancona, Ronnie. 1994. *Time and the Erotic in Horace's* Odes. Durham, NC: Duke University Press.
Barber, Daniel. 2014. "Presence and the Future Tense in Horace's Odes." *CJ* 109:333–361.
Barchiesi, Alessandro. 1996. "Poetry, Praise, and Patronage: Simonides in Book 4 of Horace's 'Odes'." *CA* 15:5–47.
Bradshaw, Arnold. 2002. "Horace's Birthday and Deathday." In *Traditions and Contexts in the Poetry of Horace*, edited by Anthony J. Woodman and Denis C. Feeney, 1–16. Cambridge: Cambridge University Press.
Cairns, Francis. 1971. "Five 'Religious' Odes of Horace (I,10; I,21 and IV,6; I,30; I,15)." *AJPh* 92:433–452.
Carey, Chris. 2016. "Negotiating the public voice." In *La poésie lyrique dans la cité antique. Les* Odes *d'Horace au miroir de la lyrique grecque archaïque*, edited by Bénédicte Delignon, Nadine Le Meur and Olivier Thévenaz, 177–192. Lyon: Éditions de Boccard.
Commager, Steele. 1957. "The Function of Wine in Horace's Odes." *TAPA* 88:66–80.
Corbeill, Anthony. 1994. "Cyclical Metaphors and the Politics of Horace, 'Odes' 1.4." *CW* 88:91–106.
Davis, Gregson. 1991. *Polyhymnia. The Rhetoric of Horatian Lyric Discourse.* Berkeley: University of California Press.

Davis, Gregson. 2007. "Wine and the Symposium." In *The Cambridge Companion to Horace*, edited by Stephen J. Harrison, 207–220. Cambridge: Cambridge University Press.

Davis, Gregson. 2016. "*Festo quid potius die*: locus of performance and lyric program in Horace, *Odes* 3.28." In *La poésie lyrique dans la cité antique. Les Odes d'Horace au miroir de la lyrique grecque archaïque*, edited by Bénédicte Delignon, Nadine Le Meur and Olivier Thévenaz, 275–284. Lyon: Éditions de Boccard.

Evans, Courtney. 2023. "*Fasti Horatiani:* Horace's Augustan Appropriation of the Calendar." *G&R* 70:38–49.

Feeney, Denis C. 1993. "Horace and the Greek Lyric Poets." In *Horace 2000. A Celebration: Essays for the Bimillennium*, edited by Niall Rudd, 41–63. London: Duckworth.

Feeney, Denis C. 1998. *Literature and Religion at Rome: Cultures, Contexts and Beliefs*. Cambridge: Cambridge University Press.

Feeney, Denis C. 2016. "Horace and the literature of the past: lyric, epic, and history in *Odes* 4." In *La poésie lyrique dans la cité antique. Les Odes d'Horace au miroir de la lyrique grecque archaïque*, edited by Bénédicte Delignon, Nadine Le Meur and Olivier Thévenaz, 295–312. Lyon: Éditions de Boccard.

Foster, Margaret. 2017. "*Poeta Loquens*: Poetic Voices in Pindar's *Paean* 6 and Horace's *Odes* 4.6." In *Voice and Voices in Antiquity*, edited by Niall W. Slater, 149–165. Leiden: Brill.

Fraenkel, Eduard. 1957. *Horace*. Oxford: Clarendon Press.

Gold, Barbara K. 1993. "*Mitte Sectari, Rosa Quo Locorum Sera Moretur*: Time and Nature in Horace's Odes." *CPh* 88:16–31.

Gramps, Adrian. 2021. *The Fiction of Occasion in Hellenistic and Roman Poetry*. Berlin: De Gruyter.

Griffin, Jasper. 1997. "Cult and Personality in Horace." *JRS* 87:54–69.

Hardie, Alex. 1998. "Horace, the Paean and Roman Choreia (Horace, Odes 4.6)." *PLLS* 10:251–293.

Harrison, Stephen J. 2017. *Horace, Odes. Book II*. Cambridge: Cambridge University Press.

Harrison, Stephen J. 2004. "Lyric Middles: The Turn at the Centre in Horace's Odes." In *Middles in Latin Poetry*, edited by Stratis Kyriakidis and Francesco de Martino, 81–102. Bari: Levante Editori.

Krasser, Helmut. 2008. "Poeta triumphans. Römische Sieghaftigkeit und die Macht des Dichters im vierten Odenbuch des Horaz." In *Machtfragen. Zur kulturellen Repräsentation und Konstruktion von Macht in Antike, Mittelalter und Neuzeit*, edited by Alexander Arweiler and Bardo M. Gauly, 127–148. Stuttgart: Franz Steiner Verlag.

Lee, M. Owen. 1969. *Word, Sound, and Image in the Odes of Horace*. Ann Arbor: University of Michigan Press.

Lieberg, Godo. 1965. "Die Bedeutung des Festes bei Horaz." In *Synusia. Festgabe für W. Schadewaldt*, edited by Hellmut Flashar and Konrad Gaiser, 403–427. Pfullingen: Verlag Günther Neske.

Lissarrague, François. 1987. *Un flot d'images. Une esthétique du banquet grec*. Paris: Editions Adam Biro.

Lowrie, Michèle. 1997. *Horace's Narrative Odes*. Oxford: Clarendon Press.

Lowrie, Michèle. 2010. "Horace: *Odes* 4." In *A Companion to Horace*, edited by Gregson Davis, 210–230. Chichester: Wiley-Blackwell.

Lyne, R. O. A. M. 1995. *Horace. Behind the Public Poetry*. New Haven: Yale University Press.

Miller, John F. 2009. *Apollo, Augustus, and the Poets*. Cambridge: Cambridge University Press.

Mindt, Nina. 2007. *Die meta-sympotischen Oden und Epoden des Horaz*. Göttingen: Edition Ruprecht.

Morgan, Llewelyn. 2005. "A Yoke Connecting Baskets: 'Odes' 3.14, Hercules, and Italian Unity." *CQ* 55:190–203.

Nisbet, R. G. M., and Margaret Hubbard. 1970. *Horace: Odes. Book 1*. Oxford: Clarendon Press.

Nisbet, R. G. M., and Margaret Hubbard. 1978. *A Commentary on Horace: Odes. Book II.* Oxford: Clarendon Press.
Nisbet, R. G. M., and Niall Rudd. 2004. *A Commentary on Horace: Odes. Book III.* Oxford: Oxford University Press.
Oppermann, Hans. 1980. "Maecenas' Geburtstag." In *Wege zu Horaz*, edited by Hans Oppermann, 183–195. Darmstadt: Wissenschaftliche Buchgesellschaft.
Phillips, Tom. 2019. "Sublime Measures: Horace *Odes* 4.6." *CPh* 114:430–445.
Putnam, Michael C. 2000. *Horace's* Carmen saeculare. *Ritual Magic and the Poet's Art.* New Haven: Yale University Press.
Putnam, Michael C. 2010. "The *Carmen Saeculare*." In *A Companion to Horace*, edited by Gregson Davis, 231–249. Chichester: Wiley-Blackwell.
Putnam, Michael C. 1986. *Artifices of Eternity. Horace's Fourth Book of Odes.* Ithaca: Cornell University Press.
Rudd, Niall. 1960. "Patterns in Horatian Lyric." *AJPh* 81:373–392.
Rudd, Niall. 2004. *Horace. Odes and Epodes.* Cambridge, MA: Harvard University Press.
Rumpf, Lorenz. 2017. "Poetische Gewissheit: Liebesdreieck und Futur in den Oden des Horaz." *A&A* 63:105–127.
Santirocco, Matthew S. 1986. *Unity and Design in Horace's* Odes. Chapel Hill: The University of North Carolina Press.
Schmidt, Ernst A. 1980. "Alter Wein zum Fest bei Horaz." *A&A* 26:18–32.
Shackleton Bailey, D. R. ³1995. *Horatius Opera.* Stuttgart: Teubner.
Sutherland, Elizabeth H. 2002. *Horace's Well-Trained Reader. Toward a Methodology of Audience Participation in the* Odes. Frankfurt a. M.: Peter Lang.
Syndikus, Hans Peter. 1972. *Die Lyrik des Horaz. Eine Interpretation der Oden. Band I. Erstes und zweites Buch.* Darmstadt: Wissenschaftliche Buchgesellschaft.
Syndikus, Hans Peter. 1973. *Die Lyrik des Horaz. Eine Interpretation der Oden. Band II. Drittes und viertes Buch.* Darmstadt: Wissenschaftliche Buchgesellschaft.
Thom, S. 2008. "Celebrating the Past: Horace's *Odes* as *aide mémoire*." *Akroterion* 53:43–55.
Thomas, Richard F. 2011. *Horace, Odes, Book IV and Carmen Saeculare.* Cambridge: Cambridge University Press.
Tringali, Dante. 1995. *Horácio. Poeta da festa. Navegar não é preciso. 28 Odes latim-português.* São Paulo: Musa Editora.

Alain Arrault
Recovering Memory by Cumulating Calendars: Festivities at Dunhuang in Medieval China (9th–10th Centuries)

Introduction

Once called the Prefecture of Sands (Shazhou 沙州), Dunhuang 敦煌 is not an oasis like any other. Located on the Silk Road linking China to Central Asia, it was an economic, religious, and cultural crossroads of the first importance. Yet we might well have known nothing of its importance, if it were not for the discovery of over 50,000 documents – mostly manuscripts, though some printed – inside a cave that had been sealed at the beginning of the 11th century. Now dispersed among various institutions – the British Library (London), the Bibliothèque nationale de France (Paris), the Institute of Oriental Manuscripts (Saint Petersburg), Ryukoku University (Kyoto), the National Library of China (Peking), the Dunhuang Academy, etc. – the oldest date from the 5th century and the most recent from the beginning of the 11th century. This extraordinary body of documentation includes religious, literary, philosophical, and political texts, as well as monastic administrative archives, and offers a window onto the reality of the lives of the inhabitants of this oasis (Fig. 1).

The history of Dunhuang is tumultuous: it was successively occupied by the Tibetans (c. 781–848), then taken back under the control of "governors" who declared themselves chiefs of the Loyal Army (Guiyi jun 歸義軍). The first of these "governors" came from the Zhang 張 (851–910) family; later they came from the Cao 曹 (914–1036) family. At this time the power of the Tang (618–907) was fragmenting, while that of the Northern Song (960–1127) was only slowly establishing itself. Under these circumstances, and over the course of numerous wars and varied alliances, the governors began, despite a façade of allegiance, to intermittently declare their independence.

Amongst the documents found are some fifty locally-made calendars, covering the period from the 9th to the 10th centuries. In large part based on the official Chinese calendars produced in the capital – at least from what little we know of this official production – they are annual and hemerological: their most salient feature is the day-by-day indication of propitious activities. In this they contrast with the

Note: Translation into English by Alice Crowther.

Open Access. © 2024 the author(s), published by De Gruyter. This work is licensed under the Creative Commons Attribution-NonCommercial-NoDerivatives 4.0 International License.
https://doi.org/10.1515/9783111366876-005

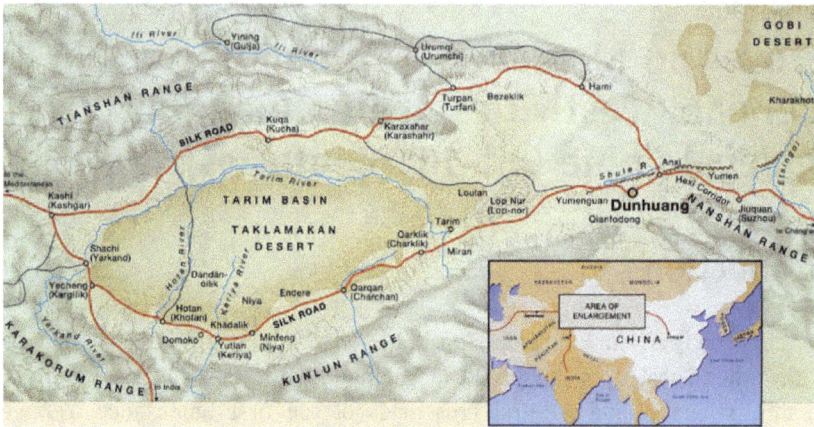

Fig. 1: Dunhuang and its surroundings. By Xuan Jiao. Creative commons license.

calendars of Medieval Europe, which were "perpetual" and liturgical, with each day dedicated to a saint.[1] Festivities occupy a relatively limited place in calendars from Dunhuang and, for the most part, mirror the festivals prescribed in the capital. However, here and there some local particularities are apparent. To counter the necessarily evanescent nature of these festivities, we need to untangle the threads of Chinese history, identifying continuities and discontinuities established over centuries, and complete this with *in situ* documents: the calendar of the days of leave of officials, a literary calendar of festivals, and the annual accounting calendars of Buddhist monasteries and of the central administration of Dunhuang. These sources can lend substance to our understanding of how the great festivals were celebrated and, furthermore, allow us to discover local cults and entertainments. It is through combining the diachronic and synchronic approaches, and the accumulation of concrete facts, that the memory of the – many and colourful – festive activities of this town in the middle of the desert may yet be recovered.

The Festivals of the Annual Calendars

Festivals – ceremonies, cults, or rituals – invariably occupy an intermediate register between the purely calendrical and hemerological portions of calendars, a po-

---

[1] On calendars from Dunhuang, see Arrault and Martzloff (2003). For a comparison with European calendars, see Arrault (2021, especially 86–90).

sition which lends them increased visibility. Eleven in number in the most complete calendars, they are mainly moveable and solar. Only three are lunar and take place on the same date each year: New Year's Eve, New Year, and the Day of Man (see Tab. 1).

These festivals are almost exclusively concerned with divinized natural phenomena and the great civilising heroes, with the exception of the Offering to the Founders, which was for historical figures such as Confucius (551–479) and his disciple Yan Hui. Apart from the Sacrifice of Opening the Springs and the Sacrifice to the Rivers, all these festivals are attested under the Han Dynasty (206 BCE–AD 220), the great age of the systemization of the rituals of official religion. This does not mean that calendrical holidays underwent no modifications during the centuries that followed their first institution. In the Tang (618–907) dynasty alone, important changes took place in the periods before and after the Kaiyuan era (714–742) reform. The compilation of the Rituals of the Kaiyuan Era (*Kaiyuan li* 開元禮) marked a decisive step in this domain however, and this held true even in Dunhuang, despite the fact that it was a region very open to local and non-Chinese influences. Finally, it is of note that in the calendars from Dunhuang, which cover the period from the beginning of the 9th to the end of the 10th centuries, two new holidays appear in the early 10th century, the Day of Man and the Sacrifice to the Rivers.

New Year's Eve, New Year, and the Day of Man

New Year's Eve (*suimo* 歲末) and New Year (*shousui* 受歲) were, as they are everywhere, festivals marking the passage from one year to the next. In China the first consists in a purification rite and a great exorcism. In Dunhuang it was called *qu'nuo* 驅儺, "drive out and welcome". Abundant literary descriptions of this exorcism, for the most part highly versified, are found in manuscripts from Dunhuang. It appears to have taken place both in public buildings, in the homes of officials, and in the most modest private houses. Processions formed, with Zhong Kui 鐘馗 and Baize 白澤 at their head, respectively the neutralizer and the hunter of demons, charged with expelling and pacifying the spirits of the five directions. Although these processions were Chinese, they did not fail to stop and pay their respect at the Mazdean altars erected by Dunhuang's very influential Sogdian population.[2] Children – both boys and girls – belting out well-known songs played an important role in these singing and dancing troops. These were both exorcistic

---

2 On this subject, see below pp. 80 ff.

Tab. 1: Festivals mentioned in the most complete calendars found at Dunhuang.

Name of Holiday / Date/month	"Reception" of the year, beginning of the year (shousui 受歲 suishou 歲首)	Day of Man (Renri 人日)	First Tilling (Jitian 藉田)	Sacrifice of Opening the Springs (Qiyuan ji 啟源祭)	Sacrifice to the Earl of the Winds (Ji Fengbo 祭風伯)	Offering to the Founders (Dian 奠, Shi-dian 釋奠)	Cult to the God of the Soil (She 社)	Sacrifice to the Rivers (Ji chuanyuan 祭川原)	Sacrifice to the Master of the Rains (Ji Yushi 祭雨師)	End-of-year La festival (La 臘)	End of the year (suimo 歲末)
993/I–III		I/7	I/22	I/23	I/12	II/19	II/20	III/20			
989/X–XII										XII/20	XII/29
986/I–XII	I/1	I/7	I/6	I/7		II/9 VIII/1	II/10 VIII/2		III/28	XII/11	XII/30
982/I–V	I/1	I/7	I/19	I/20	I/9	II/15	II/16	III/20	IV/11		
956/I–XII (Preface)			I/6	I/7		II/5 VIII/7	II/6 VIII/8			XII/11	
926/I–XII			I/23	I/24	I/25	II/1 VIII/4	II/2 VIII/5	III/8	III/28	XII/11	

and propitiatory rituals, and talismans and coloured ribbons were hung up on doors to ward off epidemics, illnesses, and other disasters from the inhabitants for the year to come.³ After this moment of "evacuating the old" at the end of the preceding year, the New Year festival, an event which took place continuously over several days – each day bringing its own lot of ceremonies, rituals, and celebrations – could begin. Attested from the 3rd century C.E., the Day of Man (renri 人日) was also part of this festive cycle.⁴ The first seven days of the year were associated with, respectively, the cockerel, the dog, the pig, the goat, the ox, the horse, and man. They formed a time apart, symbolising the process of nature's renewal and culminating in the Day of Man on the seventh day.⁵ A work from the 6th century records that on the seventh day of the first month a dish made from seven sorts of vegetables shaped in human form was prepared, and sculpted figurines were hung on folding screens and in the hair.⁶ From the Tang onwards, an eighth day dedicated to cereals was added to the list, and this list also came to serve as the base for a method of prognostication for the year to come.⁷ Although it is not listed as one of the official holidays, an entire paragraph is devoted to the Day of Man in the "Annual Festivals" chapter of the literary encyclopaedia *Yiwen leiju* 藝文類聚 (Collection of Literature Arranged by Categories), composed in 624. In Dunhuang itself it is absent from the first calendars throughout the 9th century and only appears in the calendars around 945, when P2661 V° records a propitiatory rite involving the consumption of red beans: seven for men and thirteen for women. This frugal collation was supposed to guarantee a year free from illness.⁸

---

3 See Tan (1998, 392–427). This work, often cited in this article, is a true "bible" for knowledge of the festivities which took place at Dunhuang.
4 See *Yiwen leiju* 藝文類聚, chap. 4, Shanghai, Shanghai guji chuban she, 1982, p. 60, citations from Jia Chong 賈充 (217–282) and from Li Chong 李充 (c. 326–342).
5 See *Weishu* 魏書, chap. 104, Beijing, Zhonghua shuju, p. 2325; *Bei Qi shu* 北齊書, chap. 37, Beijing, Zhonghua shuju, p. 485; *Beishi* 北史, chap. 56, Beijing, Zhonghua shuju, p. 2028.
6 *Jing Chu suishi ji* 荊楚歲時記 (*Yizhu* 譯注, n. p., Hubei renmin chuban she, pp. 25–26).
7 See *Sishi zuanyao* 四時纂要, chap. 1, 1a–1b (Zhengzhou, Henan jiaoyu chuban she, 1994, p. 187). A similar system, but based on correlations between the first twelve days of the year and the twelve months, figures in the *Kaiyuan zhanjing* 開元占經 (Book of prognostications of the Kaiyuan era), chap. 111, ed. *Siku quanshu*, 4b.
8 *Yiwen leiju*, chap. 4, p. 60. For the Dunhuang propitiatory rite, see Gao (1993, 181). See also *Sishi zuanyao*, chap. 1, 5a–5b (1994, p. 189).

The First Tilling

This ceremony (Jitian 藉田), included in the *Rites of Zhou* (*Zhouli* 周禮), unfolds according to an unchanging ritual: the king, and later the emperor, personally tills the Sacred Field (*jitian*) after having made a sacrifice to the First Tiller, Shennong 神農, the "divine labourer" whose legends said that he invented agricultural tools such as the hoe, the plough, etc., and transmitted the cultivation of the five grains to mankind.[9] This act symbolically opens the agricultural season. Although the ritual itself remained unchanging until the Tang, the same is not true of its date, which was sometimes in the first and sometimes in the second month.[10] As for the day, while preference seems to have been given to a day with a *hai* 亥 branch, – an option retained by the Tang emperors – this was not a strict rule.[11] In the Dunhuang calendars, the date is in fact the first *hai* day after the first day with the stem *xin* 辛 to follow the solar node *lichun* 立春 (Beginning of Spring).[12] However, other documents give the lie to this apparent unanimity, notably P2481 where it appears as a ceremony held in the second solar month.

The calendar for 834 mentions this festival under the name Shigeng 始耕 (Tilling's Beginning), which also appears in the 451 calendar.[13] In 900 and 901, the administrative accounts record an outlay of fifty sheets of rough paper to make paper-money for offerings to the gods for this festival (P4640 V°).

---

9 *Zhouli* 周禮, chap. 4, "Tianguan – Zhongzai" 天官 – 冢宰 (ed. *Shisan jing zhushu* 十三經注疏, Beijing, Zhonghua shuju, 1983, pp. 662–663). For a study of the ceremony of the First Tiller during and before the Han, see Bodde (1975, 223–241).
10 Under the Liang (502–557), for example, it always fell in the second month, on the basis that the ceremony had taken place in the month marked by the *mao* 卯 branch under the Yin and Shang dynasties (16th–11th centuries BCE). See *Wenxian tongkao* 文獻通考, chap. 87, Beijing, Zhonghua shuju, 1986, p. 788.
11 In the Chinese calendar, the years, months, and days are marked by a binomial of sinograms, derived from an ordered combination of a series of 10 sinograms (*jia yi bing ding wu ji geng xin ren gui* 甲乙丙丁戊己庚辛壬癸) called celestial stems, with a series of 12 sinograms (*zi chou yin mao chen si wu wei shen you xu hai* 子丑寅卯辰巳午未申酉戌亥), called earthly branches, thus forming a cycle of 60, called the sexagesimal cycle. To determine the date of festivities, a day marked with a specific stem or branch could be chosen. In this case, *hai* is the 12th sinogram of the earthly branches. – In 712 and 759, the First Tilling took place on a day with a *wu* 戊 stem and first a *zi* 子, then a *yin* 寅 branch; see *Jiu Tangshu* 舊唐書, chap. 5, Beijing, Zhonghua shuju, p. 119, and chap. 6, p. 161. It should also be noted that during the Yuanhe (84–86) era, a day with a *yi* 乙 stem was chosen.
12 This rule is attested in the *Songshu* 宋書, chap. 14, Beijing, Zhonghua shuju, p. 354. The calendars for 858 and 993 diverge from it.
13 See Deng (1989, 114). During the Han, the preferred term was Shigeng, but the expression Kai jitian 開藉田 ("opening" the sacred field) can also be found.

The Sacrifice for Opening the Springs and the Sacrifice to the Rivers

These two festivals, which appear in the calendars around the year 900, remain enigmatic: we have no precedents for them at our disposition and local sources only permit guesswork. This absence might mean that they are indigenous festivals. Left out by Tan Chanxue in his study of the annual festivals of Dunhuang, the Sacrifice for Opening the Springs (Qiyuan ji 啟源祭) only appears in calendars, where it is fixed in the first month, on the first day with the branch *zi* 子 (term *kai* 開) to follow the solar node *lichun* (Beginning of Spring).[14]

As for the Sacrifice to the Rivers (Ji chuanyuan 祭川原), the 928 preface indicates that it took place on a propitious day before or after the median node of the third month (*guyu* 穀雨 Grain Rain).[15] This is confirmed by the calendars and by the expenditure accounts for 900, 901, and 905.[16] According to Tan Chanxue, this cult was modelled on the offerings to rivers and mountains, which go back to antiquity.[17] It would thus seem to have been, as with sacrifices for the Master of the Rains and the Earl of the Winds, a simplified version of the official rites performed in the capital, designed for use in the prefectures and districts.

The sacrifices to the Earl of the Winds and the Master of the Rains

Venerated since antiquity, the Earl of the Winds and the Master of the Rains enjoyed the status of imperial cults under the Qin (221–206) and the Han. These cults were also kept at the district and commandery level. In 317 altars to these gods were ordered to be erected in all districts, to be situated near the altars of the God of the Soil and the Divine Labourer.[18] From the Sui (581–618) onwards, sac-

---

14 See National Library of China, BD 14636 V° (928).
15 Apart from its division into 12 lunar months, the Chinese year is also divided into 24 solar periods, or 24 nodal breaths (*jieqi* 節氣), each corresponding to more or less 15 days. Each solar month is determined by two "nodes", an initial node and a median node, the latter indicating the middle of the month.
16 See P4640 V° and S3728. The criteria for fixing the exact day remain unclear.
17 Tan (1998, 133–136). Another hypothesis holds that this festival commemorated an event which took place in the Dunhuang region during the reign of Emperor Xuanzong (r. 712–755); see Lu (1986, 422, note 96). The story is recounted in S5448 and in the *Taiping guangji* 太平廣記, chap. 420, Beijing, Zhonghua shuju, pp. 3423–3424. As tempting as it may seem, there is no factual basis for this association.
18 *Suishu* 隋書, chap. 7, Beijing, Zhonghua shuju, p. 141.

rifices to the Earl of the Winds (Ji Fengbo 祭風伯) and the Master of the Rains (Ji Yushi 祭雨師) were fixed as taking place, respectively, on the first day with the branch *chou* 丑 after the *lichun* (Beginning of Spring), and on the first day with the branch *shen* 申 after the *lixia* 立夏 (Beginning of Summer). These dates remained in use during the Tang. The cult of these two great deities of official religion is particularly well-documented in the Dunhuang manuscripts.[19]

The Offering to the Founders and the Cult of the God of the Soil

The particularity of these celebrations is that they take place twice each year. Under the Han, the Offering to the Founders (Dian or Shidian 釋奠) took place in the spring and in the autumn and was for the founding figures of Confucianism, principally the Duke of Zhou (r. c. 1042–1035 BCE) and Confucius. Under the Sui, the date for the prefectures and districts was fixed as the first day with a *ding* 丁 stem of the second and eighth months. In 740 the Tang took over this date, including for the capital. In Dunhuang the Offering to the Founders took place in the prefectural and district schools, which contained temples and statues (P2005). It is interesting to note that the ritual protocol followed directives promulgated by the central government, as a manuscript records the disappearance of meat offerings from the Tibetan period (c. 786–848), in conformity with an imperial decree of 731 forbidding blood sacrifices, which were to be replaced by offerings of wine and dried meat.[20]

The cult of the God of the Soil (She 社) is one of the oldest and most celebrated cults of Chinese religion. It was practiced at all levels of the empire, and its dates varied until the Northern Wei (386–534) definitively imposed the first day of the *wu* 戊 stem of the second and eighth months.[21] The 450 and 451 calendars and those of Dunhuang allow us to specify that it was the *wu* days situated the closest to the median solar nodes of the months in question (the Spring Equinox, *chunfen* 春分, for the second month and the Autumn Equinox, *qiufen* 秋分, for the eighth month).[22] In Dunhuang an altar of comparable dimensions to that described in the

---

[19] See Tan (1998, 44–48, 136–140). The most relevant documents are P2005, P3896 V°, S1366, S1725 V°, and S5747.
[20] See S1725 V° and P3896 V°. On the Offering to the Founders at Dunhuang, cf. Gao (1986, 240).
[21] The Northern Wei stipulated this date in 399, see *Yiwen leiju*, chap. 5, p. 86, and *Wenxian tongkao*, chap. 82, p. 746.
[22] However, the 986 calendar deviates from this rule for the Autumn She. For the 450 and 451 calendars, see Deng (1989, 114).

Kaiyuan li was set up in the prefecture and in the districts.²³ The lists of offerings to be buried on the days of the festival do not include blood sacrifices. However, an administrative text, which enjoins against using taxes to defray the costs of the ceremony, does mention the purchase of an ox.²⁴ Documents relating to worship associations in Dunhuang (professional and neighbourhood associations, including Buddhist associations) often specify the dues to be paid to participate in the great banquet (*zuoshe* 坐社) held on this occasion. These documents also underline the importance of this biannual festival for reinforcing community and family ties.²⁵

The End-of-Year Festival La

Already mentioned in calendars from the 3ʳᵈ century BCE, the End-of-Year Festival (La 臘) precedes and completes the New Year celebrations. Like the New Year, it involved a great exorcism (*danuo* 大儺, rite of purification and of the expulsion of malevolent forces). The day itself was dedicated to worshipping the ancestors and to the cult of the domestic gods, and the following days were for visits and banquets among friends and family. Under the Han, the festival was fixed in the twelfth month, in principal on the third day with the branch *xu* 戌 after the Winter Solstice.²⁶ This date would later be slightly modified, the *chen* 辰 branch being substituted for the *xu* branch, as is attested by the 450 calendar and all the Dunhuang calendars.²⁷ From the 6ᵗʰ century onwards, the official La tended to merge with that of the Buddhists who commemorated Sakyamuni's attainment of supreme perfection on the eighth day of the twelfth month.²⁸ The same can be seen in documents from Dunhuang which, in mentioning the End-of-Year festival, also freely evoke the monks' bathing and end of fasting, the lamps lit in caves and alcoves

---

23 See P2005 and Tan (1998, 102–103). The votive texts recited during the ceremony (S1725 V° and P3896 V°) are also very similar to those found in the *Kaiyuan li*.
24 S1725 V° and P3896 V° for lists of offerings and P2942 for the administrative text.
25 See Tan (1998, 106–107).
26 The rule is set out in one of the first Chinese character dictionaries, the *Shuowen jiezi* 說文解字 (Explaining Graphs and Analyzing Characters) compiled by Xu Shen 許慎 in the 2ⁿᵈ century CE (Beijing, Zhonghua shuju, 1979, p. 88). It was not always respected in Han Dynasty calendars. See Zhang (1989, 140) and *Yinwan Hanmu jiandu* (1997, 127). For an overview of end-of-year festivities in Ancient China, see Bodde (1975, 363–376).
27 This rule is laid out in the preface to the calendar for 928. The calendar for 450 places the festival on the fourth *chen* day after the Winter Solstice and not the third; see Deng (1996, 362).
28 See *Jing Chu suishi ji* (Yizhu, p. 133).

for Buddhist deities, and making medicines. The same is still true in the region today.[29]

The Festivals of the Calendar of Days of Leave

An imperial decree from 740[30] indicates the days of rest allocated to "outer officials" (*waiguan* 外官) – defined in opposition to the "inner officials" (*neiguan* 内官), who carried out their functions within the imperial palace (see Tab. 2[31]). This decree also appears in a manuscript found at Dunhuang – albeit leavened by some gestures towards autonomy from the capital – which seems to show that it was respected at the local level. The first thing to note is that the total number of these days of leave adds up to around 100 days, in other words almost a third of a year, a length which is surprising for a political regime with no knowledge of labour laws![32] As well as the institutional days of rest – one day off every ten days and fifteen days during the fifth and ninth months – the other holidays coincide with the dates of well-attested festivals, whether national or local. The most important un-worked days fall at New Year and the Winter Solstice, with seven days for each, and for the first the addition of a supplementary day the I/7 (7th day of the first month) and the I/15 (15th day of the first month),[33] respectively for the Day of Man, discussed above, and for the Lantern Festival (the lighting of lanterns), which marked the end of the New Year celebrations. Evidently, the Winter Solstice is not counted among the festivals of the annual calendar as such, but

---

29 See Tan (1998, 365–376).
30 This decree was recopied at Dunhuang, see P2504.
31 Apart from a few days, they are normally noted simply as dates. However, I have added the names of the festivals with which they were associated in brackets, following the indications given in the "Annual Festivals" section of the Encyclopaedia of Propaedeutic Notes (composed 728), see *Chuxue ji* 初學記, "Suishi xia" 歲時下, Beijing, Zhonghua shuju, 1985, pp. 63–86.
32 For comparison, today in France, if we count weekends, bank holidays (10), and the five weeks of annual leave, the average approaches 140 days of rest a year. However, the daily working hours in Medieval China are not known...
33 The New Year cycle seems to conclude on the last day of the first lunar month. Called *huiri* 晦日, dark or black day, it corresponds to the dark moon, that is to say the last crescent of the waning moon. It is also the year's first "last" day of the month. Although it had already been celebrated for several centuries, under the Tang it gained greater official recognition. Assimilated to the III/3 and the IX/9, it was a day of celebrations during which the emperor conferred rewards on servants of the state. It was also a day of purification on which, by custom, clothes were to be washed under running water, and on which a ritual for the expulsion of "indigence" (*song qiong* 送窮) was performed, notably by burning used clothing. To the best of my knowledge, however, no document relating to this festival has been found at Dunhuang.

rather features as one of the 24 periods of the solar year. This moment came to be so synonymous with the shift from the *yin* period of cold and hibernation to the beginning of *yang*'s emergence, and of rewarming and the progressive awakening of nature, that it was sometimes regarded as the true New Year. The Summer Solstice, which symbolizes the peak of the year's *yang* period and of the extreme heat and announces the birth of *yin* and the encroaching cold, was certainly endowed with less importance, meriting only three days of leave; it nevertheless also marked a crucial moment of shift in the seasonal year. Divided among three moments after the Summer Solstice and the beginning of autumn, the days of the three heat-waves belong to the same category: mentioned in the calendars as calendrical periods, they are intended to designate the hottest moments of the year, times for performing propitiatory rites to ward off the disasters and illnesses inherent to periods of extreme heat. The Cold Food festival and the festival of Clear Brightness follow one upon the other and are often confused. The Cold Food festival traditionally involves extinguishing all "fires" and thus eating only cold food for three days: this extinguishing is in fact a sort of renewal of the fire just before the spring.[34] It was often accompanied by banquets, singing, dancing, and walks in Dunhuang's surroundings. As for the Clear Brightness, also a solar period, it was a festival for the dead: homage was rendered to ancestors by sweeping their tombs and making offerings to them, etc. The La festival and the spring and autumn worship of the God of the Soil are entirely integrated into the annual calendar, although with a notable difference in status as the first warrants three days of leave and the second only one.[35] Other days, for instance the fifth day of the fifth month, or the seventh day of the seventh month, fall on dates fixed by the lunar calendar and correspond to traditional festivals observed nationally and at Dunhuang. The first, known as Duanwu 端午 (beginning of the fifth month), is to honour the memory of the poet-patriot Qu Yuan 屈原, who committed suicide by drowning in the 3rd century BCE; the second, also called the Night of Sevens (*qixi* 七夕), refers to the myth of the Oxherd and the Weaving Maid, two stars, but also a man and an immortal female united through marriage bonds: they are punished for this unnatural union by only being allowed to meet one day of the year, the seventh day of the seventh month, which today has become a sort of Chinese Valentine's Day. The ninth day of the ninth month is among those dates imbued with a very strong symbolic force: as nine is a *yang* number, its doubling is potentially extremely propitious.[36] A variety of documents from Dun-

---

34 Bodde (1975, 296, 299).
35 See above, pp. 66–68.
36 Therefore this festival would later come to be known as the Double Yang (*chongyang jie* 重陽節) festival, or the Double Nine.

huang – associative, literary, accounting – mention invitations among friends to celebrate this occasion; the contemplation of chrysanthemum blooms in memory of the poet Tao Yuanming 陶淵明 (365?–427);[37] drinking an alcohol with apotropaic properties derived from the Sichuan Pepper plant, and then compensating for its acrid taste by consuming a sweet alcohol made from fermented millet and chrysanthemum stems and leaves; climbing mountains to enjoy the view and consume wheat-cakes. As well as being a popular holiday, this moment was also an opportunity for the local administration to organize a banquet with dancing and music. Finally, on this propitiatory day, the deities of water-edges were not overlooked and thanks was offered to them.[38] In opposition to these joyous celebrations, the first day of the tenth month, which coincides with the first month of winter, demanded prudence and circumspection. The *jiehuo* 戒火 ritual, which was held on this day, was a ritual for preventing fires caused by starting to use heating. With the arrival of the cold, it was customary to offer winter clothes to those close to oneself and to one's elders,[39] and to make do with a frugal meal of a soup made from cereal-based vermicelli, and on this day the monks would hold a fasting ceremony (*zhai* 齋).[40]

Tab. 2: Days of leave for officials not serving in the Imperial Palace (according to an imperial decree from 740).

Name of the Festival	Date (lunar month/day)	Number of days of leave
First Day 元日	I/1	7 days (3 days before, 3 days after)
Winter Solstice 冬至	XI	
Cold Food 寒食	III, 105 days after the Winter Solstice, or two days before the solar period of Clear Brightness	4 days
Solar period of Clear Brightness 清明	III, 15 days after the Spring Equinox	

---

[37] It is said that on this day the poet, having to forego alcohol, found comfort in contemplating chrysanthemums.
[38] Tan (1998, 303–310).
[39] Tan (1998, 321–324). This festival is sometimes metaphorically designated as the festival of clothes-giving (*shouyi jie* 授衣節). Among the 30 days of holiday allocated to officials, the 15 days in the ninth month were probably intended to be in preparation for this day. In parallel to these gifts somewhat later testimony indicates that paper funerary clothing was also burned for the dead, who needed to take measures against the cold too.
[40] On this ceremony, see below pp. 72 ff.

Tab. 2: Days of leave for officials not serving in the Imperial Palace (according to an imperial decree from 740). *(Continued)*

Name of the Festival	Date (lunar month/day)	Number of days of leave
Summer Solstice 夏至	V	3 days (1 day before, 1 day after)
La festival 臘	XII	
7th day of the 1st month 七月七日 (Day of Man 人日)	I/7	1 day
15th day of 1st month (Lighting lanterns 燃燈)	I/15	
Last day [of the first month] [月]晦	I/29 or I/30	
Cult of the God of the Soil in Spring and Autumn 春秋二社	II and VIII, around the Spring and Autumn Equinoxes	
8th day of the 2nd month 二月八日	II/8	
3rd day of the 3rd month 三月三日 (festival of the First Si 上巳)[41]	III/3	
5th day of the 5th month 五月五日 (festival for the Beginning of the 5th month 端午節)	V/5	
Days of the three heat-waves 三伏日	VI, VII	
7th day of the 7th month 七月七日 (the Night of the Sevens 七夕)	VII/7	
15th day of the 7th month 七月十五日 (Avalambana 盂蘭盆)	VII/15	
9th day of the 9th month 九月九日 (重陽節)	IX/9	
1st day of the 10th month	X/1	
Leave 休假	Every 10 days	
Leave for agricultural work 田假 and giving clothing 授衣假[42]	V and IX	15 days in each of these months

---

41 During the Han dynasty, this festival involved a rite of purification through ablutions held on the first day with the branch *si* 巳 in the first decade of the third month. After the Han, the date of this festival was fixed as the 3rd day of the 3rd month.

42 In the capital, all advanced students, exam graduates, and the students of the Imperial Academy were due leave in the 5th month when fields were sown, and in the 9th month for the giving of clothes. See *Xin Tangshu* 新塘書, "Xuanju zhi shang" 選舉志上, Beijing, Zhonghua shuju, p. 1161.

All of these days of leave are linked either to solar periods or to dates from the lunar calendar and are all historically well-attested and entirely integrated into popular custom. Despite their official nature in both the annual calendars and the calendar of days of leave, it would be a mistake to see the festivals linked to these days as "secular" holidays. In fact, they all have an evidently cultic and religious dimension: performing rituals and rites, addressing and thanking the gods, commemorating the founders of civilization or divinized heroes. In parallel to these official calendars, liturgical calendars did also exist, established by the two major religions of China, Daoism and Buddhism. As well as participating in their own way in these official festivals, these two faiths also organized their own religious activities, in which communities participated without devotional or sectary tendencies necessarily coming into play. The calendar of days of leave gives us two indications that the Buddhist liturgical calendar, in particular, was taken into account: the 15th day of the seventh month is identified in the Encyclopaedia of Propaedeutic Notes as the day of Avalambana's festival; and the eighth day of the second month, not included in the encyclopaedia, is in fact a Buddhist holiday.

Literary Description of Festivals at Dunhuang

The manuscript S2832 is a composite document, incorporating models for both *zhai* rituals and letter-writing.[43] In Ancient China, *zhai* 齋 designated a period of fasting and abstinence – a purification – before a ritual. In Buddhism, it designated not only a fast taking the form of a spartan banquet, but also rituals and rites performed on this occasion. In general, *zhai* comprised prayers, liturgies of sutra rotation, funerary ceremonies, and dedicative and festive rituals.[44] In the manuscript in question, these *zhai* rituals are associated with the funerals of husbands, wives, monks, etc., and also with entirely celebratory and Buddhist rituals, and with a hymn in praise of Sakyamuni. As for the model letters, they give patterns for protocolary letters and mention both monthly weather phenomena and the festivals celebrated throughout the year. It must be underlined that, with the exception

---

43 See manuscript S2832, held by the British Library. This manuscript has been entirely transcribed in Hao (2016, 240–312). I would like to thank Zhang Chao and Wu Nengchang for obtaining copies of this text for me.
44 On this subject, see Ding (2020).

of two documents at the end of the manuscript,⁴⁵ the texts are models and do not allude to any specific events or people. Here we will naturally be concerned with the festivals evoked in a literary manner (see Tab. 3).

Tab. 3: Festivals mentioned in the manuscript S2832.

Name of the Festival	Date, Name, and Dedication	Principal Activities
Yue zheng yuan ri 月正元日	I/1, first day of the first month	
Shiwu ri 十五日	I/15	"Dragon" lanterns are hung in trees; dances, banquets, singing; at night: lighting the thousand lanterns
Er yue ba ri 二月八日	II/8, flight of the future Buddha from his palace	Men and women erect canopies and hang up banners⁴⁶...
Er yue shiwu ri 二月十五日	II/15, allusion to the physical death (parinirvana) of Sakyamuni, which happened underneath a tree	
San yue san ri 三月三日	III/3, the day shangsi 上巳 (the first si day); a ritual dedicated to the god of water	Exorcism ritual
Si yue ba ri 四月八日	IV/8, birth of the Buddha; his first seven steps were accom-	Washing the statues of Buddha

---

45 These two texts both mention rituals for the attainment of merit, one involving gifts of effigies and copies of sutras by a certain Huangfu and his wife, and the other a hymn in praise of Sakyamuni, by one Zhao who also gifted effigies.

46 The setting-up of canopies and banners alludes to the "white canopy" (baisan 白傘) ceremony during which Buddhist statues were sheltered under a sort of parasol and carried in procession to the four corners of the town. In the same way, banners decorated the ritual areas where psalmodies and sutra readings etc. were performed. On the baisan, which were part of a ritual involving the rotation of sutras, lighting lanterns, a procession of statues, impressing the Buddha's footprints on wet sand (or clay), etc., see Wang (2007). According to Yu Xin 余欣, "Shengcheng zhizao yu shouhu: Dunhuang ansan xuancheng yishi zhong chuangsan de gongneng" 圣城制造与守护：敦煌安伞旋城仪式中幢伞的功能 (Making and Guarding Sacred Spaces: Function of Dhavaja Parasol Used in Dunhuang Ritual of City-Parading with White Chattraa), the ceremony of setting up the canopy, along with the procession that led the participants to the town's four corners, was a way to sacralize the territory, to distinguish between inside and outside, and to drive out all calamities. On the impressing of the Buddha's footprints (yin sha fo 印沙佛), also associated with making moulds of Buddhas (tuo fo 脫佛) and stupas (tuo ta 脫塔), Kunsang Namgyal-Lama's PhD dissertation is extremely interesting: Namgyal-Lama (2013, especially 26–29, 79–81, 92–93).

Tab. 3: Festivals mentioned in the manuscript S2832. *(Continued)*

Name of the Festival	Date, Name, and Dedication	Principal Activities
	panied by the flowering of the lotus	
Wu yue wu ri 五月五日	V/5, Duanwu festival (the beginning of Summer), allusion to the dismissal of Qu Yuan; also called "the day of longevity and contrition"	
Qi yue qi ri 七月七日	VII/7, night of the encounter between the Oxherd and the Weaving Maid on the Milky Way	
Qi yue shiwu ri 七月十五日	VII/15, the festival Avalambana, the day when Mulian feasted the Buddhist deities to whom, through avarice, his mother had not offered food; she cannot avoid the "eight difficulties" of existence and thus finds herself in the infernal world of the "hungry ghosts"	All families organize banquets (of offerings) to compensate for the failing of Mulian's mother
Jiu yue jiu ri 九月九日	IX/9, day of the flowering of the chrysanthemums; the day when Huan Jing 桓景 (c. 25–220) and his family climbed a hill and drank chrysanthemum alcohol to escape from the plague; the day on which the poet Tao Yuanming 陶淵明 (c. 365–427) admired chrysanthemums in his retreat	
Dongzhi ri 冬至日	XII, the Winter Solstice; the day on which the gnomon's shadow is at its longest; the year's node changes, it was the first month in the calendar of the Zhou; the Fu hexagram (Renewal) gives birth to a *yang*...	
La yue ba ri 臘月八日	XII/8, the day on which monks bathe to purify themselves and eliminate suffering	

Tab. 3: Festivals mentioned in the manuscript S2832. *(Continued)*

Name of the Festival	Date, Name, and Dedication	Principal Activities
La ri 臘日	XII, the day Jiaping 嘉平;[47] the day on which Zhang Liang 張良 (262–186 BCE) made an offering to Huang Shigong 黃石公, who revealed the arts of war to him; the day of the Buddha's enlightenment	Thanksgiving sacrifice to the gods and spirits
Suichu ri 歲除日	The last day of the year; the year in course finishes during this night	

The first thing to strike the eye is the Buddhist colouring of these festivals. No fewer than six of them are intimately linked to this religion, which had arrived from the West. Among the eight main stages (*ba xiang* 八相) that punctuated the Buddha's appearance among living beings, five took place in this world: birth, flight from the palace, enlightenment, preaching, realization of nirvana.[48] Here his birth is marked on the 8th day of the 4th month, his flight on the 8th day of the 2nd month, his enlightenment in the 12th month, and his physical death on the 15th of the 2nd month. In reality these dates have little grounding in historical fact. However, for our purposes at least one of them – the flight from the palace on the 8th day of the 2nd month, signifying Sakyamuni's conversion to a new spiritual life, far from the wealth and luxury of his palace – does explain why a day's leave was given to officials on this date in particular. The Avalambana – whose Chinese transcription (*yulan* 盂蘭) would appear to come from the Sanskrit and Pali term "odana" ("cooked rice") with the addition of the Chinese term *pen* 盆 (a basin) and therefore designates "a rice bowl" for offerings[49] – is also typically Buddhist. Here this festival is linked to the famous story of Maudgalyayana, alias Mulian 目連 in Chinese: his mother, despite the instructions of her son, did not make offerings to the Buddhas; when she died, because of this failing, she was reborn in the infernal world of "hungry ghosts" (*preta*). Through filial piety Mulian used all means at his disposal to free his mother from this hell, beseeching the Buddha,

---

[47] Jiaping was the name given to the 12th month in Ancient China, later replaced by *la yue* 臘月 (month of the *la*).
[48] See Wang-Toutain (1996, 73–74).
[49] See under the entry "ullambana" in *The Princeton Dictionary of Buddhism*, Princeton: Princeton University Press, 2014, p. 936.

who, in the end, ceded to his pleas: he instituted the Avalambana during which, through making offerings to the community of monks, those who have had a bad rebirth may be reborn in a better "world". Mulian's mother was finally reborn in paradise. The same goes for the bathing of the monks on the 8th day of the 12th month, known as the *la ba* 臘八 (the festival *la* of the 8th), constituting a period of retreat, purification, contrition, and repentance for the Buddhist community, beginning on the XII/1 and finishing on the XII/8 with the reading of sutras and offerings. At Dunhuang, this festival led to well-soused banquets of monks and nuns![50] This festival is directly followed by the communally celebrated *la* held in the same month, in this text described as honouring the enlightenment of the Buddha, and which would normally coincide with the *la ba*. The other festive moments correspond with what we have already seen, with however some historical precisions: as well as the poet Tao Yuanming, Huan Jing is mentioned for the chrysanthemum festival on the IX/9; Zhang Liang, a famous strategist born in the 3rd-century, is mentioned for the *la ri*...

The Festivals According to the Calendars of Annual Accounts

We know, from many documents Buddhist and otherwise – prayers, copies of sutras made in order to earn merit, circulars from worship associations, dedications from those who commissioned them on isolated votive paintings or on cave-walls – that Buddhist communities not only followed their own liturgical calendar assiduously, but also actively participated in various "pagan" festivals. However, there is no more eloquent proof of this than that furnished by the calendars of annual ac-

---

[50] This was not the only occasion on which the Buddhist community partook of a sort of beer, made with one or more of the local cereals (millet, panic, wheat or barley). According to Éric Trombert, in the monasteries one drank a lot and on all occasions: "at the great annual festivals evidently, but also to celebrate the return of a colleague, or to see him off on a journey, in honour of officials, craftsmen, musicians, or other visitors, after the community activities, or while doing the monastery accounts. They drank privately, but also in gatherings in the public house, and the monasteries themselves financed these sorts of assembly for their monks or nuns, for craftsmen, or for local dignitaries" ("lors des grandes célébrations annuelles bien sûr, mais aussi pour fêter le retour d'un collègue, ou pour lui souhaiter bon voyage, pour honorer des fonctionnaires, des artisans, des musiciens, ou d'autres visiteurs, après les travaux communautaires, ou en faisant les comptes du monastère. On buvait entre soi, mais on se réunissait aussi au cabaret, et les monastères finançaient eux-mêmes ce genre d'assemblées en faveur de ses religieux, d'artisans ou de petits notables", Trombert (1999, 172).

counts kept by the monasteries of Dunhuang. Éric Trombert counts four manuscripts from the 10th century, which come from a major Dunhuang monastery, the Jingtu si 淨土寺.[51] The annual accounts of the monastery were solemnly presented, most often at the beginning of a new year, by the accountant-monk in charge of the annual balance. The particularity of these accounts is that they include only foodstuffs or transformed products, with no mention of currency. Clearly, it is through its expenditures that the real implication of a monastery in the annual festivals is apparent (see Tab. 4)[52]. *Grosso modo*, these expenditures involve quantities of wheat (or barley), millet, and soybean; various flours made from wheat or barley; hempseed oil; crabs; and finally, to a lesser extent, pieces of cloth and sheets of paper. The festivals and ceremonies for which these expenditures were intended needed preliminary preparation and generally took place over the course of several days, which is clear proof of the monks' investment in "pagan" festivals like the New Year, the Cold Food Festival, and the Winter Solstice. These accounts also show that the most important Buddhist festivals, in terms of expenditure, were held on the 8th day of the 2nd month and the 15th day of the 7th month, each of which days gave officials the right to a day's leave. Once again, the porosity of the boundary in China between what we designate by the misnomers religious and secular life – in reality a single whole belonging to a total cultic regimen – is apparent here. The first of these dates, the 8th day of the 2nd month, commemorates the flight of Sakyamuni from his palace, as we have seen, but, according to sources from Dunhuang, could also be the day of his birth.[53] It involved rituals carried out both within and outside of the monastery, processions of statues in and around the town accompanied by musical instruments and dances, communal banquets (denoted as "spartan"), masquerades to

---

51 My discussion of these annual accounts from Dunhuang is entirely based on Éric Trombert's article (Trombert 1996).
52 This table synthesizes the different festivals for which expenditures were noted in the annual calendars for various years from the monastery Jingtu si, and is based on the material in É. Trombert's article (Trombert 1996).
53 The date of the Buddha's birth was a source of confusion in China: it was placed either on the 8th day of the 2nd month or the 8th day of the 4th month as attested by S2832. Some prayers from Dunhuang seem to designate the 8th day of the 2nd month as the moment of the future Buddha's conversion, although in the end they remain very vague. As Françoise Wang-Toutain has justly remarked: "The only thing we can be sure of, thanks to the monastery accounts, is that the great annual holiday for the Buddha's birthday took place on the 8th day of the 2nd month in Dunhuang" ("La seule chose que nous puissions affirmer, grâce aux comptes de monastères, c'est que la grande fête annuelle du Buddha avait lieu à Dunhuang le 8e jour du 2e mois"), see Wang-Toutain (1996, 89).

ward off plagues, etc.[54] The second date, which we have already encountered under the name Avalambana, also involved the participation of Daoists and was generally carried out for the dead (Fig. 2), in particular *malemorts* – souls condemned to wander because of their sins or because of the sins of the living towards them.[55] This link was so close that it was also called the ghost festival (*guijie* 鬼節).[56] It is notable that these two moments coincide with two major moments in the agricultural calendar, the first with the sowing of seeds in the spring, and the second with the autumn harvests.[57]

Tab. 4: Festivals celebrated by the Buddhists at Dunhuang, according to the Calendars of Expenditures (10th century).

Festival	Date
New Year	I/1
Lantern Festival (*randeng* 燃燈)	I/15
Birth of Sakyamuni, Sakyamuni's flight from the palace	II/8
Cold Food (*hanshi* 寒食)	III, 105 days after the Winter Solstice
Food for the Buddha (*foshi* 佛食)	Spring
Spring Banquet	Spring
Avalambana (*yulanpen* 盂蘭盆)	VII/15
Autumn Banquet	Autumn
Food for the Buddha	Autumn
Winter Solstice	XI
12th month ceremonies	XII

---

54 Françoise Wang-Toutain describes the unfolding of the festival of the 8th day of the 2nd month with precision on the basis of the preparations made for it – these included the illumination of monasteries and the nearby painted caves – in her article "Le sacre du printemps. Les cérémonies bouddhiques du 8e jour du 2e mois", Wang-Toutain (1996, 79–88).
55 The "malemort" in classical antiquity and medieval Europe has also attracted much attention, see Charlier (2009) and Bayard (2008).
56 On this ghost festival see, among others, Teiser (1988).
57 Trombert (1996, 71).

Fig. 2: Votive image of the goddess Guanyin. On the left is a Buddhist monk, on the right the donor who commissioned this painting for his deceased younger brother on the 15th day of the 7th month, in 901. British Museum VII 15, painting on silk. © The Trustees of the British Museum.

Miscellaneous Festivals and Entertainments

"Foreign" Cults

Dunhuang was an oasis where varied populations lived side by side: Chinese, Tibetans, Uyghurs, Khotanese, Sogdians… Commercial and cultural intermediaries between the worlds of Central Asia and China, where their presence is attested as early as the 2nd century, by the time of the Tang dynasty the Sogdians could boast a centuries-long presence on Chinese territory. This is amply attested by tombs excavated at the capital at Xi'an and at Taiyuan and by written testimony of their presence almost everywhere in China.[58] They played an important role in the history of the Tang dynasty. As well as their role as intermediaries with the Byzantine Empire and the world of Indian Buddhism, two facts will suffice to demonstrate their influence: the infamous An Lushan 安祿山 (703–757), a general in the Chinese army who, in the 8th century, instigated the rebellion that was to destabilize the Tang dynasty right up to its final fall in 907, was in fact born to a Sogdian father and a Turkic mother; and, in Dunhuang in particular, the influence of the Sogdians was so great that the locally-produced calendars were the first to adopt the idea of the week, previously unknown in China, and the names they gave to the days of the week derived from the Sogdian.[59] The Sogdian community's main temple was situated to the east of the town of Dunhuang; paintings of Mazdean deities have also been found at this site.[60] It is therefore unsurprising that the Sogdians were actors in the religious life of the oasis, as manifested in regularly organized festivities, among other things. We know this not from the annual accounts of Buddhist monasteries, but from the accounts of the local administration. Paper expenditures for the years 899, 900, and 901 include gifts of paper for the *sai xian* 賽祆. *Sai* designated a thanksgiving ritual and *xian* designated Mazdeanism, and the expression seems to correspond to the Zoroastrian ceremony Āfrīnagān.[61] The quantity given, on several occasions over the course of a year (see Tab. 5), is almost always the same: 30 sheets of paper-for-painting (*huazhi* 畫紙), which one supposes was meant for painting Mazdean deities, this

---

58 Trombert (2003, 231–241).
59 Arrault and Matzloff (2003, 100–101).
60 Grenet and Zhang (1996, particularly 175–180).
61 Grenet and Zhang (1996, 181–182). Pénélope Riboud has shown that in China the character *xian* was used to qualify the religious practices of other *hu* (barbarians), including Turks and Indians and religious customs issued from the steppes, as well as for the Sogdian religion: Riboud (2005, 73–91).

number corresponding to the 30 deities of the Zoroastrian pantheon.[62] Incidentally, one of the entries for these expenditures specifies that these papers were offered on the occasion of a procession to the Eastern Lake and its surroundings. To these gifts of paper should be added gifts of beer[63] in 887 and 964 (?), another foodstuff, which seems to be flour, and lamp-oil.[64]

Tab. 5: Gifts of paper and beer for the thanksgiving ceremony for the *xian* 祆 deities.

887 P3569	899 P4640	900 P4640	901 P4640	964? Dunhuang Institute, P2629
		I/13 (paper)	I/11 (paper) II/21 (paper) III/3 (paper)	
IV/14 (beer)		IV/8 (paper) and IV/16 (paper)	IV/13 (paper)	IV/20 (beer)
	VII/25 (paper) X/5 (paper)	VII/9 (paper) X/9 (paper)		VII/10 (beer)

Daoist Cults

The festivities held at Dunhuang were not confined to the worship of Buddhist and "foreign" deities. There were also the cults and religious activities of the Daoists and religious practices whose particularities derive in great part from the local economy.

Under the Tang dynasty, Daoism underwent considerable development, both theologically and institutionally. Sibling to and rival of Buddhism, Daoism comes

---

62 The number of 30 sheets-for-painting is used in other contexts, it is therefore not certain that it corresponded to an exact number of deities to paint. It may rather have been a conventional "grant".

63 According to Trombert (1999), the alcoholic drink (*jiu* 酒) in question was brewed and fermented from millet or from wheat/barley, and should therefore be classified as a beer rather than a wine or a distilled alcohol. Other specialists estimate that the word "beer" does not correspond exactly to Chinese beverages. According to Tang Mi, the base material and process are very similar to beer production, but the difference with beer is that Chinese alcohol does not go through the malting stage: Tang (2023, 27–28). The best translation might be "fermented grain alcohol". For reasons of consistency, however, I have kept the word beer in this article.

64 Grenet and Zhang (1996, 185 n. 36) mention in particular the manuscripts S1366 – a register of the expenditures of the Dunhuang central administration – for expenditures of cereals, oils, and food, and S2474.

into play at three nodal moments of the calendar year in particular. These are designated by the expression The Three Origins (*san yuan* 三元) and take place in the 1st, 7th, and 10th months. The Officials of Heaven, Earth, and the Waters (*san guan* 三官) intervene in succession. In the 7th month the Official of Earth (Diguan 地官) descends to examine the good and bad actions of the living, and the 15th day of this month is understood to be dedicated to both ancestors and *malemorts*. It gave rise to ceremonies which were carried out concomitantly with the Buddhist Avalambana festival.[65] At Dunhuang, while Daoist sources – in the main part copies of liturgical and alchemical texts – are abundant before the mid-8th century, they are very rare after this date. Against 700 texts before this date, there are only around 70 manuscripts after it, for the most part ceremonies for funerals and protecting homes, and treatises on divination and exorcism techniques.[66] Only two community cults linked to Daoism are attested.

On the VIII/10 a gift of 30 rough sheets, for making paper money, was made for the thanksgiving ritual consecrated to the deity Zhang *nülang* 張女郎 (P4640). Miss Zhang seems to be the daughter of Zhang Lu 張魯 (?–216?), the grandson of Zhang Ling 張陵, founder of the Daoist current known as the Five Bushels of Rice, which was at the origin of the Heavenly Masters order that the Zhang family still hereditarily lead to this day. On Mount Nülang 女郎山 in the Mian District 勉縣, not far from Hanzhong, which Zhang Lu occupied for over 20 years, a cult was offered from at least the 3rd century to a Zhang Yulan 張玉蘭, identified as a daughter or sister of Zhang Lu. An anthology of *mirabilia* from the Northern Song recounts that, while she was washing her clothes at the foot of the mountain, a white fog enveloped her body and she became pregnant. Ashamed, she committed suicide, but took the precaution of asking her serving-maid to open her belly after her death: the maid thereby discovered two small dragons, which she took and placed in a river. After Zhang *nülang*'s burial, several dragons assembled on the site of her grave and a river then formed before it.[67] In Chinese mythology, dragons are associated with rivers and streams. It is therefore unsurprising that a prayer from Dunhuang addressed to the rain mentions, among others, Zhang *nülang*, in a way the mother of dragons, and that, as well as the Buddhist monks who performed a *zhai* ritual, local ritual specialists were involved in carrying out this prayer at Xuanquan 懸泉 (the Hanging Spring, a site near Dunhuang) (S6315).[68] Throughout the

---

65 On the role of Daoism and the Avalambana, see Teiser (1988, 35–42).
66 Wang (2004, 9–16).
67 See *Taiping guangji* 太平廣記 (Extensive Records from the Era of Great Peace, compiled between 976 and 984), chap. 418, Beijing, Zhonghua shuju, 1986, pp. 3401–3402.
68 The poem "Qingming deng Zhang nülang shen miao" 清明登張女郎廟 by Su Qie 蘇㐲 – found copied out in manuscripts from Dunhuang – evokes the poet's visit to the temple of Miss Zhang,

year rituals performed on the edges of rivers, ponds, or dikes are frequently evoked. Several account-books attest regular expenditures of sheets of paper, foodstuffs, and lamp-oil for thanksgiving ceremonies for the deities of the edges of water.[69] One of them is named in a model prayer: Yunü *niangzi* 玉女娘子, Lady Jade Maiden (S343). Jade Maiden, the alter ego of the Golden Lad (Jintong 金童), belongs to the Daoist pantheon as a serving-maid for the immortals. She is also called Sunü 素女 (the Pure Maiden) and Qingnü 青女 (Azure Maiden), and she controls weather phenomena such as frost, hail, snow, storms...[70] The model prayer in question situates the ritual action on the River Duxiang 都鄉河, which in fact is a term for a canal dug less than ten kilometres southwest of Dunhuang.[71] Some specialists think that Miss Zhang and the Jade Maiden are one and the same deity, others affirm to the contrary that they are two separate deities: thus Miss Zhang is linked to a specific sanctuary, whereas the Jade Maiden is present in all watery places.[72] Regardless, both are female deities who control water and rain, primordial resources in an oasis.

Agricultural Cults

These resources were above all of concern for agriculture, which depended on irrigation water and rain for good harvests. It its therefore unsurprising that a festival was dedicated to the god of Green Sprouts (Qingmiao shen 青苗神). It took place in the 4th month, in 899, 900, and 901 on, respectively, the 9th, 16th, and 13th day of the month, and the local administration allocated 50 sheets for making paper money for this deity (P4640), as well as foodstuffs, flour, and oil (S1366). The 4th month is in fact the month in which young sprouts of wheat or barley

---

which is situated in the present-day district of Qianyang 千陽 some 150 km to the west of the capital Chang'an (modern-day Xi'an) during the festival of Clear Brightness, in the 3rd month. See Tan (1998, 129–130).
69 Gao and Zhao (2005, 70). Account-book P4640 mentions three or four sacrifices performed on the water-edge in 899, 900 and 901, including, evidently, that for Miss Zhang. However, on these occasions the Jade Maiden is not mentioned.
70 Gao and Zhao (2005, 68–69).
71 Gao and Zhao (2005, 69–70). Another thanksgiving ritual, dedicated to the deity Qinglei 青雷 (Azure Thunder), was performed in the 8th month (S6306). The identity of this deity is not very clear: was it the god of Thunder (Leishen 雷神), who was worshipped at the Spring and Autumn Equinoxes (and more specifically during the 8th month for the latter equinox), or the Azure Maiden, Qingnü, another name for the Jade Maiden? This second hypothesis seems the most plausible, as among other things the Jade Maiden controlled storms.
72 This is the thesis of Gao and Zhao (2005, 73).

emerge from the ground, taking the form and size of "a horse's ear", as the *Qimin yaoshu* 齊民要術, a treatise on agriculture and home economics from the 6th century, elegantly describes them. These sprouts urgently need to be hoed and weeded so that they may become fine ears in a few months' time. Grapes are another typical product of Western China. At Dunhuang, the vines were covered with sandy earth during the winter to protect them from the cold and, at the end of spring and the beginning of summer, they were released from this protective membrane, and one hoped that the first visible seeds would become fine bunches of grapes a few months later. This, the 4th month, was the moment chosen for thanking the deity or deities for making these seeds: in the Nansha vineyard 南沙園, which belonged to the local administration, they were offered 5 portions of "fine dishes",[73] 50 "barbarian" cakes,[74] over three bushels of flour, and oil (S1366).

As Dunhuang was a focal point for trade and exchange between Central Asia and China, horses and camels were of the first importance there. According to the official ritual regulations, a sacrifice was to be offered to the deity Horse-Ancestor (Mazu 馬祖) in the 2nd month. This deity is sometimes glossed as a star, Tiansi 天駟 or Tianma 天馬 (Celestial Horse), but in the minds of the populace of Dunhuang was probably more associated with the flesh-and-blood animal. A stable had been founded at Dunhuang at the beginning of the Tang dynasty. With the passage of time a cultic association for the Horse God (*mashe* 馬社) and finally a stud (*mayuan* 馬院) were also established. An extract from the calendar of expenditures of the Office of Firewood (Chaichang si 柴場司) from 955 shows that on II/23 the Office paid out three faggots of tamarisk and thorns for a thanksgiving ritual for the Horse God (S3728). On the 22nd day of a 4th month, a first account mentions an offering of beer to the god when the horses left for pasture (Dunyan 001); in a second account, it is after the 25th day of the 4th month that offerings are made for the departure for the pastures; a groom, who this time led camels out to pasture, is paid 7 portions of food for the gods (*shenshi* 神食), cakes, flour, and oil (S1366), for

---

[73] The Chinese term is *xigong* 細供, literally "fine offerings", and its exact meaning is cause of great perplexity. According to different sources, it always appears at the head of a list of offerings or gifts, whether in the case of diplomatic relations with the representatives of neighbouring countries, religious activities, or compensating the administrators and craftsmen who had carried out building work. It was followed by what would seem to be "lesser offerings", listed in order of importance. It therefore probably consisted in a set of refined dishes, whose value was greater than that of the other foodstuffs. It was worth 1.9 *sheng* 升 of flour (1 *sheng* = 6 decilitres), while a barbarian cake was worth 0.5 *sheng*, according to Tan (1998, 225). For *xigong*, see Sheng (1996, 101–104) and Gao and Dai (1998, 83).

[74] The term which we are translating imperfectly as "cake" is the character *bing* 餅 in Chinese. *Bing* is a generic term denoting cakes, raviolis, and stuffed buns... *Hubing*, "'barbarian' cakes", covered everything which came from the West, generally from Persia. See Trombert (1996, 67–68).

the same cult; the same happened on the 12th day of an intercalary 3rd month of a non-specified year (S2474). During the 5th and 6th months, the administration again dipped into its coffers for sheets-to-paint, paper money, and beer. The most impressive expenditure, however, is for the great ritual banquet organized in honour of the Horse God, held on the VI/7 both at the beginning of the 10th century and in 947. Nothing was skimped on: in flour equivalents, the first account mentions 7 piculs and 6 bushels,[75] enough to feed around 380 people for one day (P2667); the second no less than 12 piculs and more than 5 bushels, enough to feed 600 people for one day (P2641)! In the 8th month, the expenditures come back to normal again: on the VIII/3, 1 bushel of beer is allocated (P2629), and the ritual takes place not outside, as was the case with the other festivities, but inside the stud: in mid-autumn the time has come to bring the horses back inside, in accordance with a calendrical rhythm which dictated that the horses should be let out at the Spring Equinox and brought back in at the Autumn Equinox.[76] Worship of the Horse-god took place at the same time as worship of the caprid,[77] to whom half a jar of beer was allotted. The concomitance of these two cults is strange, as the two animals were not of equal status. Caprids are animals intended to feed humans, or perhaps to be offered in sacrifice; the horse is not so destined. The central administration raised around 700 heads of caprids and their mid-autumn fate was fixed: most of them would be butchered and provide a store of meat to get through the winter. Offering a cult to the caprid thus served to get around the Buddhist ban on slaughtering animals by ritually guaranteeing the salvation of the animal who, through this ritual, could escape from its animal condition and be reborn among humankind. By making the animal a god, the transgression of the butchers is absolved. This ambiguity did not exist for the horse: close to man, for whom he carried out many services both economic and military, he was also his playmate.

Games and Cults

From the Han dynasty onwards, mounted acrobatics were part of horse training. Called, metaphorically, "the monkey's rides" (*yuanqi* 猿騎), these acrobatics involved all sorts of feats: standing up or lying down on the horse; sitting backwards; holding various objects in one's hands; balancing, etc. These sorts of gymnastics,

---

[75] A picul (*shi* 碩) was worth 10 bushels (*dou* 斗) or 100 *sheng* 升. A picul is equivalent to around 60 litres.
[76] Tan (1998, 290–291).
[77] The Chinese term used is *yang* 羊, and it is not always evident if sheep or goats are meant. I have therefore preferred to stick to the generic term "caprid".

and thus the art of breaking in horses, were part of military training in China too. A famous collection of jottings dealing with life at Kaifeng 開封, the capital of the Northern Song, describes horseback acrobatics as part of the manoeuvres demonstrated by soldiers in the 3rd month.[78] The same seems to have been true in Dunhuang, at least if we give credence to wall-paintings from Cave no. 61, which depict a man kneeling on a galloping horse and holding up a metal plaque over his head; another man on horseback who seems to be leaning down to pick something up from off the ground; a third drawing an arrow while on horseback and another driving four horses in hand (Fig. 3)...[79] A monastery account from the 10th century records an offering of enough millet to brew six bushels of beer for a horse-trainer[80] in the 4th month (P4906). Also in the 4th month, between 976 and 984, this time in a record from the administration's accounts, the gods of horseback acrobatics are thanked for their protection in order to avoid dangerous falls and at the same time "fine dishes", cakes, flour, and oil are offered to the acrobats (S1366). The quantity of food offered indicates that at least 10 acrobats were to be rewarded.

The game of polo seems to have reached China by the early years of the Tang dynasty, perhaps from Persia or Tibet. There was such a craze for the game that in the 10th century Emperor Taizong 太宗 of the Song established a protocol for the competition that was played in front of the palace in the 3rd month. The emperor would hit the first ball, to the sound of drums, and then take the second hit, which signalled the opening of the game, to be played by princes and high officials.[81] The horse was not the only mount used for polo: there are also several accounts of donkeys being used,[82] and of women as well as men – all, of course, belonging to the

---

78 *Dongjing menghua lu* 東京夢華錄 (Dreams of the Splendours of the Eastern Capital, 1187), 7, "Jiadeng Baojin lou zhujun cheng baixi" 駕登寶津樓諸軍呈百戲 (Driving to the Baojin Pavillion where the soldiers present a hundred games). The author, Meng Yuanlao 孟元老, exiled to South China after the invasion of the North by the Jurchen, recalls the urban life of the capital of the Northern Song with nostalgia.
79 The wall paintings from Cave no. 61, which is located at Mogao 莫高, appear to date from the 10th century. At this site in the near suburbs of Dunhuang several hundred Buddhist caves were painted or sculpted from the 4th century onwards.
80 A scene from Cave no. 290 shows a trainer facing a kneeling horse.
81 Tan (1998, 170). On the history of polo from the Tang to the Song, see Liu (1985).
82 P1477 includes a funeral prayer addressed to a donkey "Ji lü wen" 祭驢文, with the phrase: "As you were not born into a family of soldiers, you did not have the strength to play polo." The *Dongjing menghua lu*, 7, records that in the 3rd month a hundred people mounted on donkeys played polo before the imperial palace. Cited by Tan (1998, 170).

Fig. 3: Flyers on horseback... Mural painting in Mogao Cave No. 61, Dunhuang. © Dunhuang Academy.

aristocracy – playing.[83] The best players enjoyed a certain degree of prestige and excelling at the game could help with one's career, especially in the military.[84] When Zhang Yitan 張議潭 (?–860), the governor of Dunhuang, went to the capital Chang'an to pledge allegiance to the Tang dynasty, he was singled out by the emperor for his talent on the polo field (P3556). At Dunhuang, the third son of the governor Zhang Huaishen 張淮深 (831–890), Zhang Yanshou 張延綬, was said to be an excellent player and the best in the region (P2568). The polo competition at Dunhuang took place on a plot of land near the town's central gate (P3773), in the 4th month. The administration's accounts record foodstuffs given to ten "villages" – a term here designating the teams in the competition, representatives of the nearby villages and neighbourhoods (Dunyan 001, S1366). There is also a record of over a bushel of flour being exchanged in order to give a monk named Kong 孔, master of the Law and doctrine (falü 法律), a polo stick (S1366). A model letter mentions

---

[83] The tomb of a Madame Cui 崔氏, who died in 878, contains the skeleton of a donkey, which archaeological analyses show to have been not a pack animal but a mount for playing polo. See Hu et al. (2020).

[84] See, for example, the biography of Zhou Bao 周寶, the husband of Madame Cui (see the preceding note), whom the emperor promoted to the rank of general because of his talent as a polo player. After he had lost an eye in a polo match, he was then appointed to a post in the Board of Public Works. Cited in Tan (1998, 169).

polo matches (S5636) and poems copied out at Dunhuang dwell on Homeric-sounding matches (S2049, P2544).

As well as polo, the nobility and the elite also sought amusement in hunting with birds-of-prey. From Chinese Antiquity, the traditional – and strongly ritualized – hunt was carried out with birds-of-prey on gauntlets and with dogs. The bird of preference was a goshawk (*accipiter gentilis*), known in Europe as the Northern Goshawk. The Uyghur population had such a reputation as hunters, tamers, and suppliers of these creatures that in China their official name was "returning falcon" (*huihu* 回鶻, *hui*回). It was the Uyghurs who ran the shops in the neighbourhood that was entirely dedicated to the sale of these birds at Kaifeng.[85] The goshawk was highly prized: it made up part of the tribute sent to the emperor of China by the governors of Dunhuang. In 866 Zhang Yichao 張議潮 (799–872), imperial commissioner of Dunhuang, sent Emperor Yizong 懿宗 4 goshawks (or 4 goshawk couples) from the Ganjun 甘峻山 mountains, a region in central Gansu renowned for its birds-of-prey, as well as two horses and two Tibetan women, for his birthday. They were economically valuable, but more important still was their symbolic value: the goshawk represented savagery tamed by civilization and thus incarnated the perfection of Chinese sovereignty.[86] Evidently, great attention was paid to these birds and they were fully integrated into the calendrical rhythm of festivities. They appear at two moments of the year: the moment for setting out to hunt goshawks in the seventh month and the return of the hunters between the middle of the ninth month and the beginning of the tenth.[87] When the hunters set out in pursuit of goshawks, in 899 on the VII/22, they were given 50 sheets-for-painting intended to be offered to the gods in order to facilitate the hunt (P4640); and on a VIII/29 and a VIII/30 beer (P2629), also for the gods (*shenjiu* 神酒). These expenditures came from the public purse, as the "falconers" had been dispatched by the central administration to carry out this task. On different dates, the IX/17 and 18, and a IX/30 (P2629), beer was again given to the falconers, but this time to reward them for their effort and their hunting, which must have been suc-

---

[85] *Dongjing menghua lu*, 2, "Dongjiao lou jiexiang" 東角樓街巷 (Roads of the Eastern Corner's Pavilion). There was a birds-of-prey neighbourhood in the town of Dunhuang as well (S6981). On "falconry" under the Tang, see Edward H. Schafer's study (Schafer 1958), which reviews all the available Chinese sources and remains a classic on the subject.

[86] Mayo (2002).

[87] Composed in the 10th century, the *Youyang zazu* 酉陽雜俎 devotes several pages to hunting goshawks and to the nets used to capture them, etc. According to this work, the best moment to capture them in the "inner" territory was the VII/20. The period between the first and the last decades of the 8th month was a little less favourable, however this period was the best moment for hunting them in the "outer" territories. This period seems to correspond with the time for hunting migrating goshawks, who were still young but capable of flying and catching prey.

cessful to different degrees as there are wide discrepancies between the quantities of beer awarded to different hunters (varying from 90 decilitres to 36 litres)!

Conclusion

This overview of festivities at Dunhuang, from the 9th to the 10th centuries, could be continued at greater length, but what has already been presented seems sufficient to justify some general observations. If we accept that culture includes, but also goes beyond, the limited domain of liturgy, or of religion in the wider sense of the term, then it is clear that the cultural memory in question here is in fact more cultic than cultural. The main pretext for these festivals was almost always a deity, whether founders of civilization or divinized heroes, gods from the Buddhist or Daoist pantheons, or the "little" gods of local society. Nothing escaped the cultic sphere, whose frontiers are evidently porous: there is no truly profane world to be opposed to a sacred world, and less still is there a secular world in opposition to a religious world; devotees and actors from both spheres take part in festivities that are not a priori intended for them. Officials underwrite Buddhist rituals, Buddhists pay great attention to so-called official festivals, and it seems highly probable that the local population took part in all these forms of festivity, including those said to be the reserve of the elite such as polo and hunting with birds-of-prey, indiscriminately.

However, it is only through the juxtaposition of different types of calendars that this cultic idiosyncrasy, and the porosity of the boundaries between social classes, have come to light. Looking at just one of these calendars would only have provided a glimpse, correct but lacunar, of the festivities held in the oasis: with just the liturgical calendar of the Buddhists, for example, we would only have seen that they celebrated the different moments of the historical Buddha's life, while the great attention paid to some of these moments in particular would not have been apparent; we would also have overlooked the involvement of monks and nuns in some of the "official" festivals such as the Cold Food festival or the Clear Brightness festival. And we would have completely missed the Daoist deities regularly worshipped and known nothing of the presence of Sogdians in the oasis, horseback acrobatics, or polo and goshawk-hunting.

The memories here have been recovered through an accumulation of calendars: local official calendars, the calendar of the leaves of absence of officials, literary calendars, and, perhaps most importantly, calendars of expenditures, whether from the central administration or the monasteries. These recovered memories are based on two kinds of calendar: prescriptive calendars, which organize time and the events to come at the beginning of the year, and recapitulative calendars, which record what has happened over the course of a year. Two forms of memory thus combine, one turned towards the future, the other looking back at the past; one offering a promise for the future, the other a final report-card. Simultaneous access to these two forms of memory gives us an incomplete but realistic image of the festivities, entertainments, and games that diverted the inhabitants of an oasis in the 9th–10th centuries.

References

Arrault, Alain, and Jean-Claude Martzloff. 2003. "Calendriers." In *Divination et société dans la Chine médiévale. Etude des manuscrits de Dunhuang de la Bibliothèque nationale de France et de la British Library*, edited by Marc Kalinowski, 85–211. Paris: Bibliothèque nationale de France.

Arrault, Alain. 2021. "Les activités quotidiennes dans les calendriers de la Chine medieval." In *Les calendriers d'Europe et d'Asie. De l'Antiquité à la diffusion de l'imprimerie*, edited by Arrault, Alain, Guyotjeannin, Olivier, and Perrine Mane, 71–104. Paris: Ecole nationale des chartes.

Bayard, Florence. 2008. "Pourquoi les morts reviennent-ils." In *Les Vivants et les Morts. Littératures de l'entre-deux-mondes*, edited by Arlette Bouloumié, 1–29. Paris: Imago.

Bodde, Derk. 1975. *Festivals in Classical China*. Princeton: Princeton University Press.

Charlier, Philippe. 2008. *Male mort: morts violentes dans l'Antiquité*. Paris: Fayard.

Deng, Wenkuan 鄧文寬. 1989. "Dunhuang guli congshi" 敦煌古曆叢識 (Dunhuang Ancient Calendars). *Dunhuang xue jikan* 1:107–118.

Deng, Wenkuan 鄧文寬. 1996. "Dunhuang liri zhong de nianshen fangwei tu jiqi gongneng, 敦煌曆日中的年神方位圖及其功 (The Function and Location of the Annual Spirits in Calendars from Dunhuang)." In *Duan Wenjie Dunhuang yanjiu wushi nian jinian wenji*. Beijing: Shijie tushu, 254–259.

Ding, Yi. 2020. *Divine Transactions: the Transformations of Buddhist Communal Liturgies at Dunhuang (8th – 10th centuries)*. PhD Dissertation. Stanford University.

Gao, Guofan 高國藩. 1993. *Dunhuang minsu ziliao daolun* 敦煌民俗資料導論 (Introduction to Dunhuang Folklore Materials). Taipei: Xinwenfeng.

Gao, Mingshi 高明士. 1986. "Tangdai Dunhuang de jiaoyu" 唐代敦煌的教育 (Education in Tang Dynasty Dunhuang). *Hanxue yanjiu* 4.2:231–270.

Gao, Qi'an 高啟安 and Suo Dai 索黛. 1998. "Tang Wudai Dunhuang yinshi zhong de bing qiantan – Dunhuang yinshi wenhua yanjiu zhi er" 唐五代敦煌飲食中的餅淺探 – 敦煌飲食文化研究之二 (The Cake: A Kind of Food of Dunhuang during the Tang and Five Dynasties Periods). *Dunhuang yanjiu* 4:76–87.

Gao, Qi'an 高啟安 and Zhao Hong 趙紅. 2005. "Dunhuang Yunü kaoxie" 敦煌玉女考屑 (A Study of Yunü [Jade Goddess] in Dunhuang Manuscripts). *Dunhuang yanjiu* 2:68–73.

Grenet, Frantz, and Zhang Guangda. 1996. "The Last Refuge of the Sogdian Religion: Dunhuang in the Ninth and Tenth Centuries." *Bulletin of the Asia Institute*. 10:175–186.

Hao, Chunwen 郝春文 (ed.). 2016. *Ying cang Dunhuang shehui lishi wenxian shilu* 英藏敦煌社會歷史文獻釋錄 (Annotated Transcription of Documents on the Social History of Dunhuang held by the British Library), vol. 14. Beijing: Shehui kexue wenxian chuban she.

Hu, Songmei, *et al.* 2020. "From pack animals to polo: donkeys from the ninth-century Tang tomb of an elite lady in Xi'an, China." *Antiquity* 94.374:455–472.

Liu, James T. C. 1985. "Polo and Cultural Change: From T'ang to Sung China." *Harvard Journal of Asiatic Studies*. 45.1:203–224.
Lu, Xiangqian 盧向前. 1986. "Guanyu Guiyi jun shiqi yifen buzhi poyong li de yanjiu – Shishi P4640 beimian wenshu" 關於歸義軍時期一份布紙破用曆的研究 –試釋伯4640背面文書 (On a calendar of the expenditure of sheets of paper and cloth from the Guiyi jun period – An attempt at explaining P4640 V°)." *Dunhuang Tulufan wenxian yanjiu lunji* 3:394–466.
Mayo, Lewis. 2002. "Birds and the Hand of Power: a Political Geography of Avian Life in the Gansu Corridor, Ninth to Tenth Centuries." *East Asian History* 24:1–66.
Namgyal-Lama, Kunsang. 2013. *Les tsha tsha du monde tibétain : études de la production, de l'iconographie et des styles des moulages et estampages bouddhiques.* PhD thesis. Université Paris-Sorbonne.
Riboud, Pénélope. 2005. "Réflexions sur les pratiques religieuses désignées sous le nom de *xian* 祆." In *Les Sogdiens en Chine*, edited by Étienne de La Vaissière and Éric Trombert, 73–91. Paris: EFEO.
Schafer, Edward H. 1958. "Falconry in Tang times." *T'oung Pao* 46:293–338.
Sheng, Chaohui 盛朝暉. 1996. "'Xigong' kao" 細供考 (Examination of the expression "xigong"). *Dunhuang xueji kan* 2:101–104.
Tan, Chanxue 譚蟬雪. 1998. *Dunhuang suishi wenhua daolun* 敦煌歲時文化導論 (Introduction to Dunhuang Festivals). Taipei: Xinwenfeng.
Tang, Mi. 2023. "Étude sur l'alcool et sa fabrication à partir d'un traité de la dynastie Song, le *Beishan jiujing* 北山酒經 de Zhu Hong 朱肱 (début du XIIe siècle)", PhD dissertation. Aix-Marseille université.
Teiser, Stephen. 1988. *The Ghost Festival in Medieval China.* Princeton: Princeton University Press.
Trombert, Éric. 1996. "La fête du 8e jour du 2e mois à Dunhuang." In *De Dunhuang au Japon. Etudes chinoises et bouddhiques offertes à Michel Soymié*, edited by Jean-Pierre Drège, 25–72. Genève: Droz.
Trombert, Éric. 1999. "Bière et bouddhisme : la consommation de boissons alcoolisées dans les monastères de Dunhuang aux VIIIe–Xe siècles." *Cahiers d'Extrême-Asie* 11:129–181.
Trombert, Éric. 2003. "Un sujet d'actualité : les Sogdiens en Chine des Han aux Tang." *Etudes chinoises* 22:231–241.
Wang, Ka 王卡. 2004. *Dunhuang daojiao wenxian yanjiu* 敦煌道教文獻研究 (Studies on Daoist Documents from Dunhuang). Beijing: Zhongguo shehui kexue chuban she.
Wang-Toutain, Françoise. 1996. "Le sacre du printemps. Les cérémonies bouddhiques du 8e jour du 2e mois." In *De Dunhuang au Japon. Etudes chinoises et bouddhiques offertes à Michel Soymié*, edited by Jean-Pierre Drège, 79–88. Genève: Droz.
Wang, Wei. 王微 (Françoise Wang-Toutain). 2007. "Baisan gai fo mu: Han Zang fojiao de hudong" 白傘蓋佛母：漢藏佛教的互動 (Sitatapatra Interactions between Chinese and Tibetan Buddhism)." *Gugong bowu yuan yuankan* 5:98–152.
Yinwan Hanmu jiandu 尹灣漢墓簡牘 (Wooden slips and bamboo lattes from the Han tombs of Yinwan). 1997. Beijing: Zhonghua shuju.

Index

agriculture   64, 71, 78, 83 f.
altar   7, 40, 61, 65 f.
anticipation   3, 30, 40–44, 46 f., 49 f.
astronomy   2, 6, 11–25
atmosphere   6, 41, 53
audience   7, 11, 23, 28, 30, 33, 35 f., 40, 44, 48 f., 53, 55, 57

banquet   42 n. 8, 56, 67, 69 f., 72–74, 76–78, 85
beer   76 n. 50, 81, 84–86, 88 f.
birthday   43, 55, 77 n. 53, 88
Buddhism   60, 67 f., 72–82, 85, 86 n. 79, 89–91

calendar   1 f., 6 f., 11, 15, 18, 24 f., 35–37, 43, 46, 54, 56, 59–91
ceremony   40, 47 f., 60, 63 f., 67, 70, 72 f., 77 f., 80–83, 91
commemoration   4, 43, 65 n. 17, 67, 72, 77
consecration   18, 21, 23, 82
cult   11, 13 f., 25, 56, 60, 62, 65–67, 71 f., 77, 80–85, 89

dance   3, 6, 61, 69 f., 73, 77
Daoism   72, 78, 81–83, 89, 91
death   5, 27, 30–33, 36, 45, 47–49, 51 n. 31, 55, 69, 70 n. 39, 73, 75, 78, 82
decoration   3, 6, 39, 73 n. 46
Dionysia (Greater Dinoysia)   7, 35 f.
divination   82, 90

Elder Brother   14, 16, 18–22, 24
Enūma Eliš   11–12, 14
epic   11–12, 14, 28 f., 33, 53, 56
equinox   17 n. 15, 36, 66, 70 f., 83 n. 71, 85
eternity   9, 40, 46, 50, 54 f., 57
exorcism   18, 21, 23, 61, 67, 73, 82

Festivals *passim*
– aftermath of   5
– expenditure   65, 77 f., 80 f., 83–85, 88 f., 91
– food   3 f., 23, 69 f., 74, 77 f., 81, 83 f., 86 f., 89 f.
– participation in   3, 5 f., 11, 13 f., 20, 22–24, 48, 57, 67, 72, 73 n. 46, 76, 78

– preparations   3–5, 18, 27, 39, 41, 44, 46, 48 f., 51, 63, 70 n. 39, 77, 78 n. 54
– public vs. private   1 f., 39 f., 43, 46–50, 54, 61, 76 n. 50
– secular vs. religious   72, 77, 89

games   3 f., 6, 85–87, 90

holidays   23 f., 61–63, 68, 70, 72, 77 n. 53
Homer   51, 88
hymn   47 n. 22, 52, 72, 73 n. 45

Immortality   7, 36 n. 11, 40, 43, 46, 53, 55, 69, 83

kairos   50
king   11–14, 22 f., 25, 31 f., 64

Mazdeanism   61, 80
memory   5, 40 n. 3, 52, 59 f., 69 f., 89 f.
moon   11, 17 n. 15, 18, 44, 68 n. 33
music   3, 6, 39, 70, 76 n. 50, 77

new year   2, 11–25, 61, 63, 67–69, 77 f.
night   2, 16–19, 30, 36, 52, 69, 71, 73–75

offering   35, 47 n. 23, 61 f., 64–67, 69 f., 74–76, 81, 84–86, 88

politics   1 f., 7 f., 42 f., 46, 48, 55, 59, 68, 91
power   2, 31, 43, 46 n. 19, 55, 59, 91
prayer   14, 16, 18, 21, 24, 72, 76, 77 n. 53, 82 f., 86 n. 82
priest   12–14, 16–18, 21, 23, 25
procession   12–14, 23, 49, 61, 73 n. 46, 77, 81
prostitute   44 f.

rhythm   3 f., 6, 50–53, 85, 88
ritual   2, 4, 8, 10, 11–25, 47, 49, 57, 60 f., 63–73, 77, 80, 82–85, 88 f.
ritual texts   12 f., 22, 24 f.

sacrifice   6, 49, 61f., 64–67, 75, 83 n. 69, 84f.
sanctuary   27, 83
scholars   1, 12f., 17–20, 24f., 40
seasons   16, 64, 69
– autumn   66, 69, 71, 78, 83 n. 71, 85
– spring   17 n. 15, 36, 44–46, 64–66, 69–71, 78, 83 n. 71, 84f.
– summer   18, 46, 66, 69, 71, 74, 84
– winter   18, 36, 67f., 70, 74, 77f., 84f.
Secular Games   53f.
slave   42, 44, 48
stars   24f., 30, 69, 84
statues   11f., 14, 18, 22f., 66, 73, 77
sun   2, 11, 16–22, 24, 29–31, 35
symposium   40f., 43, 45f., 48, 54, 56

temple   11f., 14, 18, 20–25, 66, 80, 82 n. 68
thanksgiving   70, 72, 75, 80–84, 86

time *passim*
– cyclical   11, 15, 40, 50, 52–55, 63f., 68 n. 33
– 'Eigenzeit' (proper time)   3
– ephemerality   6, , 34, 37, 55
– everyday   1–6, 31, 39
– festive   *passim*
– fleetingness of   7, 39f., 41 n. 8, 44–49, 54f.
– human   4f., 31–34, 36, 39, 43f., 46, 50, 53, 55
– linear   17, 40, 50, 52
– sacred vs. profane   1 n. 2, 9, 89
– scheduled time   11, 15, 22, 31
– sequential   11, 20–22, 24
– short time   2, 11, 15f., 20, 22, 24f.
tradition   2, 5, 11, 17–19, 51, 53, 55, 69, 88

wine   6f., , 39, 41, 44, 48f., 55f., 66, 81 n. 63

Zoroastrianism   80f.

www.ingramcontent.com/pod-product-compliance
Lightning Source LLC
Chambersburg PA
CBHW051544230426
43669CB00015B/2714